Praise for

DAD UP!

"As always, Steve Patterson finds the unusual in the natural, the unnatural in the ubiquitous, the light in the dark and the dark in the light, then twists the whole mess into wonderfully crafted comedy that captures the weirdness that's inherent in being human. This book is a touching and very funny read. At least up to the chapter in which he mentions me. I stopped reading after that."
BRENT BUTT, creator of *Corner Gas*

"If you were hoping Steve Patterson's *Dad Up!* would make you howl with laughter, well your wish will be granted page by page. But you may not have expected his reflections on parenthood to be so thoughtful, moving, even wise. The best of both worlds. Powerful prose from a very funny rookie Dad."
TERRY FALLIS, two-time winner of the Stephen Leacock Medal for Humour

"This book should come with a READ BEFORE PARENTING sticker. It won't teach you how NOT to get punched in the testicles, but you will gain a mother-load of hilarious insights into fatherhood that superhero mums everywhere will be grateful you learned."
DENISE DO~~~~~~~~~~~~~~~~~~~~~~~~~~~~~~~tive and author of *Fearless as Possible (Unde*

DAD UP!

Also by Steve Patterson

The Book of Letters I Didn't Know Where to Send

DAD UP!

LONG-TIME COMEDIAN.
FIRST-TIME FATHER.

STEVE PATTERSON

PENGUIN

an imprint of Penguin Canada, a division of Penguin Random House Canada Limited

Canada • USA • UK • Ireland • Australia • New Zealand • India • South Africa • China

First published 2021

www.penguinrandomhouse.ca

LIBRARY AND ARCHIVES CANADA CATALOGUING IN PUBLICATION

Title: Dad up! : long-time comedian. first-time father. / Steve Patterson.
Names: Patterson, Steve, 1971- author.
Identifiers: Canadiana (print) 20200237500 | Canadiana (ebook) 20200237519 |
ISBN 9780735238350 (softcover) | ISBN 9780735238367 (EPUB)
Subjects: LCSH: Fatherhood—Humor. | LCSH: Parenthood—Humor.
Classification: LCC PN6231.F37 P38 2021 | DDC C818/.602—dc23

Book design by Matthew Flute
Cover design by Matthew Flute
Cover images: (Dinosaur) © EricFerguson / Getty Images; (mug) © GraphicTurkey

Printed in Canada

10 9 8 7 6 5 4 3 2 1

Penguin
Random House
PENGUIN CANADA

This book is dedicated to John "Slim" Patterson
for providing me with a blueprint for being a dad.

And to Nancy, Scarlett and Norah
who help me refine that blueprint daily.

Contents

Prologue

Contrary to what many books on the subject will tell you, nothing can truly prepare you for becoming a dad. And I'm not just saying this because I didn't read any books on the subject.

I've seen the expression "Any man can be a father, but it takes a special man to be a dad" on many Father's Day–themed coffee cups. Which is weird because, for one thing, it's called FATHER'S Day, not DAD'S Day. So in the interests of selling more merchandise, you would think they'd say, "All fathers are very special—especially the one holding this cup." Then again, if your Father's Day gift is a coffee cup, maybe your kids are trying to tell you something. If they really loved you, they would have bought you this book.

Not every man can be a father.

Some men can't have children. As a matter of fact, now that I think about it, *no* man can have children. A man needs a female partner—or two men need a female surrogate (of course it takes only one woman to do work that even two men can't)—so really those smug mugs have it all wrong. They should read: "No man can be a father unless he has a willing female to go through the incredibly difficult process of carrying another human being around in her belly for many months and then endure the excruciating experience of delivering that baby, which men cannot do because, compared to moms, dads are extreme wusses and largely irrelevant."

But that would be tough to fit on a mug. Even an enormous novelty one.

All of this shows how unbalanced the division of labour really is between moms and dads in the early years. Especially when it comes to the actual act of <u>labour</u>. So that message would make more sense for Mother's Day. On a well-deserved bottle of wine.

Still, there is something to be said for pointing out the difference between a father and a dad. I remember watching the old *Maury Povich Show*, a daytime talk show that regularly included paternity test segments, back in the 1990s. (There were far fewer viewing options on TV in that decade than there are now.) In these segments, Maury would interview a young woman who was the mother of a newborn or a toddler, while two or three men sat backstage looking nervous. Each man thought he might be (but desperately hoped he *wasn't*) the father of the baby. The men would then be traipsed out on stage to hear the results of the paternity tests the show had administered. (If you're having a paternity test administered by a talk show, you're already off to a bad start as a dad, BTW.) Then whichever man was revealed to be the father would react as if his life was ruined, while the others would jump around as if they'd narrowly avoided a prison sentence.

These men were not real fathers.

Or real dads.

Or real men.

Sure, technically, you become a father the moment your baby is born, but you don't really. You become a father over years of commitment, of teaching your kids valuable life lessons, of supporting your children emotionally and (as I'm currently finding out very quickly) financially. You become a father when you put family before yourself. I think I truly became a father the first time my baby girl Scarlett called me "dad." Not "dada." Babies will call anyone or anything "dada": their favourite stuffed animal, a family pet, their own reflection, and perhaps most awkwardly, sometimes your best friend, Ted. But when your child looks at you and calls you DAD, you know you've made it.

You also know that child wants you to do one of three things:

1. Buy said child something
2. Pick up said child and carry them (a long distance)
3. Wipe said child's butt

Nothing tells you your life isn't all about you anymore like request number 3 (especially when you're wiping up after number two).

But being a dad isn't all biological. To the men who step into the role of fatherhood, by becoming stepdads or through adoption (or being a dad-figure), I salute you as well. It's not an easy role to take on. Just think about one of the earliest examples: Jesus's stepdad, Joseph. Tough sandals to fill, but Joseph did all he could to dad up!

Finally, there's no "right age" to become a dad (though I would suggest you aim for sometime after your teens and before your eighties). There's also no one playbook for being a dad (though I would argue that the more you make time for play, the more fun a dad you will be). And there is no way you won't screw up. In fact, in the early days of dadhood, you *will* screw up. Multiple times. Just like your dad screwed up while raising you. And that's okay. The best dads learn from their mistakes, so in a way, the more mistakes you make, the better a dad you become! (This is something that dads who make a lot of mistakes tell themselves.)

And look on the bright side: your children probably won't remember all those screw-ups. Or one might grow up to be a comedian and write a whole book about them.

CHAPTER 1

Before I Was a Dad

I was born on April 15, 1971, the fifth son of John and Kathleen (same last name as me). My mom described my birth this way: "I was so excited that everyone in the hospital thought you were my first!" Dad said, "I'm not sure I was there for the actual birth, but I remember your mother being quite excited."

Of course, like most people, I don't remember the first few years of my life. This is probably because those of us of Irish descent are slightly drunk off our Irish mothers' breast milk for those early days. I'm not saying that all Irish moms are alcoholics—people within the extended Irish community assumed that Guinness was good for expectant mothers because of its iron content. Which could be why so many Irish people are fabulous fiction writers, but off the top of my head, I can't think of a single one who's a successful neurosurgeon.

Anyway, I came into the world as the youngest of five boys. My oldest brother, John, was already eighteen; my second oldest brother,

Larry, was sixteen; Mark was ten; and Ross, aka Ox, was five and a half but already the size of a teenager.

The Irish Catholic community would refer to me as the proper outcome of birth control; the medical community would refer to me as a mistake. I prefer to think of myself as a surprise—or as the wildly optimistic types would put it, the save-the-marriage baby. My dad sincerely believed I was immaculate. Not because I was a beautiful baby but because he had no recollection of conceiving me with my mother. (And like all children, I prefer not to recall the moment of conception either—so we are both puzzled as to how it happened.)

In any case, if I was the immaculate save-the-marriage baby, I had my work cut out for me because my parents' marriage was definitely in need of divine intervention. Even though the family had lived relatively happily in Montreal (where all my older brothers were born) for several years, things had not been going well since the move to neighbouring Ontario in 1969. This had something to do with dad's problems with authority at work, mom's ostracizing herself from family members because of depression and Larry and Mark's obsession with driving their cars too fast on the streets around our neighbourhood, which resulted in my parents being on a first-name basis with a lot of Toronto police officers.

To say things were lean in the Patterson household would be like describing the Irish Potato Famine as not quite having enough food. Ironically, though, the one thing I remember eating a *lot* of growing up was potatoes. At our house, every meal was a competition, with a bunch of growing boys fighting over each morsel of food like wild dogs over roadkill. As the youngest child, I lived in constant fear that

1. I might not get enough to eat; and
2. my brothers would eat ME when the food ran out.

This turned me into a very fast eater at a very young age—and was likely the reason my brothers nicknamed me Fast Eddie (though I still don't understand the "Eddie" part).

Even so, I remember being a pretty happy little kid.

Sure, we didn't have a lot of money and I dressed mostly in my brothers' hand-me-downs. While other kids were sporting Star Wars T-shirts, I was modelling Ross's ripped jeans. (Note: Pre-ripped jeans weren't in style at that time—nor were they the indication of affluence they inexplicably seem to be now.) But as the youngest brother, I also had the best security detail at St. Luke Catholic School in Thornhill, Ontario. While my brothers taught me to defend myself by battling back against their relentless barrage of headlocks and wedgies, they also made sure that I didn't have to defend myself against anyone other than them. This is not to say that my brothers were bullies. On the contrary. The motto my dad instilled in us was "Never start a fight, but always know how to finish one." This is easy advice to give but less easy to practise. I still find that the best way to finish a fist fight is to keep it from starting.

Anyway, before I was born, my brothers had given Dad the nickname Slim because of his runner's physique. By the time I came around, the moniker didn't really fit anymore (much like Slim's old running singlet). But I didn't really question it because I was still trying to figure out the Fast Eddie thing.

In Montreal in the 1950s, Slim was the envy of the neighbourhood. As a buyer for Eaton's department store, one of his jobs was to entertain Mr. Hockey himself, Gordie Howe, whenever the Detroit

Red Wings were in town to play the Montreal Canadiens. So it was that my dad brought Gordie home for dinner one day, having first explained in a phone call to my mother and my brothers John and Larry to tell no one about the visit. Naturally, they told everyone they knew, so when Dad and Mr. Howe arrived at the house, all the kids in the neighbourhood were lined up around the block to meet him and get autographs, which Mr. Hockey graciously provided, even though it almost made him late for the game that night.

Now, this was a really cool dad thing to do—even if I did *not* get to witness it because I was far from being born at that time. But if you, as a dad, happen to get the opportunity to bring the country's greatest sports hero home for dinner, I suggest you go ahead and do it.

Yes, things were good for the "pre-Steve" Pattersons back then. Dad had a solid job, Mom doted on her boys and there were regular trips to a cottage of some sort (must have been a rental because otherwise I would be taking my family on regular trips there today).

It was a perfect middle-class life.

Until it wasn't.

By 1969, Dad had lost his job at Eaton's and Mom had alienated her family to such an extent that there were no get-togethers with cousins, uncles, and aunts anymore. By this time my brothers Mark and Ross were on the scene. Now, it's not my brothers' fault that there were problems between my parents. It is *never* a child's fault when a marriage starts to crumble, and any parent who suggests such nonsense frankly shouldn't be a parent. But it does put tremendous stress on an already strained marriage to have young children to raise and support, especially if you're counting on those children to be the glue that holds the whole shaky thing together. That's not a kid's job.

A kid's job is to be a kid. A parent's job is to help that kid become the best person he or she can be. Period.

My parents divorced when I was eight years old, and although I know now it wasn't my fault, it sure felt like it was back then. As any child of divorced parents knows, the breakdown of a marriage is not a fun time. I mean, I suppose it could be if you have one parent trying to one-up the other with gifts and trips. But that wasn't the case in my family. I lived with my mom in Toronto and spent most of my time blocking out whatever slights about Dad she was trying to plant in my head, while Ross moved to nearby London with Slim and our dad's dad (aka Gramps). The premise should have been as funny as the show *Frasier*, but it wasn't. My older brothers, meanwhile, were out on their own by then. Lucky them.

Like the old man in *Frasier*, Gramps would sit in the living room in his favourite chair (which happened to be a lawn chair) and watch TV for hours on end, but with an interesting twist: the set wasn't turned on. He was essentially watching his own reflection in the TV screen and either wondering why he was on every channel or challenging himself to a relentless staring contest (overall record: 0 wins, 0 losses, many ties). When Gramps wasn't busy watching his own reflection, he would turn off the taps in the kitchen to make sure they didn't leak. This meant cranking them counter-clockwise as tight as they would go (he was still surprisingly strong, even though he was in his seventies). When someone went to turn on the taps again, it was like trying to pry open a manhole cover that had been welded shut. I didn't drink a lot of water in those days.

Meanwhile, back in Toronto, my living situation with my mom started out badly and went downhill from there. She lost her job at a local car dealership (along with the car that came with it) so we constantly travelled by train from Toronto back to Montreal to visit my grandmother and aunt, both of whom lived in very small apartments with a very large number of very large cats.

These train rides (which were often in lieu of attending school) were where I did a lot of my learning, so I really didn't have a grasp on many traditional subjects, like math. Yet I was able to answer the question "If a train leaves Toronto at 11:30 a.m. on a Tuesday, what time will it arrive in Montreal?" (The answer was 4 p.m. sharp if you were on the express, and 5:30 if you took the milk route. Duh.)

Mom and I spent most of those trips playing cards, and maybe if Mom's game had been poker, I would have learned a lot from her. The only game we played, though, was Crazy Eights. So all I really learned was that cards of the same suit stick together, the number two is an arsehole (because it makes you pick up additional cards), and the number eight can change anything at any time. Surprisingly, these haven't turned out to be marketable life skills. Plus, Mom always let me win. Either that or I am the best Crazy Eights player in the world (which might be the only profession less lucrative than being a Canadian entertainer).

Growing up taught me that while not all family time results in good times, and that there will be some bad memories, it's actually the happy memories that kids seem to hold on to. So whatever you can do to help make those happy memories happen is your most important job as a dad.

Oh, and the best way to start being a dad is to, wait for it, have a child.

CHAPTER 2

A Scarlett Is Born

It all really started for me on August 29, 2014. That was the day when Scarlett Sharon Patterson came into the world and yours truly became a father. I'd been warming up to the idea of fatherhood ever since my wife, Nancy, first told me she was pregnant. But a lot of things can happen during a pregnancy—many of them devastating (we had already experienced this more than once)—so I hadn't really dared to think about it until the second I heard my daughter's first cries. We were in the delivery room, and Scarlett, mere seconds old, was screaming at the indecency of being plucked from a primordial hot tub that she'd had no intention of getting out of (she was two weeks past her due date, which is about the amount of time it still takes her to get ready for a routine outing). Meanwhile I was a forty-three-year-old man feeling very much like I had just been reborn myself. In a way, I had been. Because the days of leisurely comedy creation and self-promotion that are an important part of the comedian's trade would now include the responsibility of keeping another human being alive. Jesus! I should have thought this through. What was I thinking? I'm not up to this. Is there a way to . . . put the baby back in?

"No, Mr. Patterson, you cannot put the baby back in," the fifty-something German-accented nurse replied sternly. I guess I had said my thoughts out loud. Dammit. "Now would you like to cut the cord?"

Ah, yes, the famous cord cutting. It's a tradition as old as time to make the father feel like he has really contributed to the process. Sure, Nancy had been in active labour for twenty-seven hours (including a few hours at home while I slept soundly, preparing for her to, you know, go into labour), but now it was up to Stevie Scissorhands to make this thing official.

For those who have never cut an umbilical cord (I believe this group includes my dad, even though I am one of *five* sons), let me say that it's a very surreal feeling. You're handed a special pair of scissors, then with a group of doctors, nurses and other medical professionals watching you, you proceed to make just ONE cut. It's like the ribbon-cutting ceremonies you see politicians taking part in. Only when it's done, you don't get to leave and never again care about the building you've just opened. You have to take what is on the end of that umbilical cord (your human offspring) home, where you must then keep her safe and nourished—oh, and teach her everything you know (including how to cut an umbilical cord).

I was extremely nervous. What if I screwed up and cut the cord wrong? What if I hurt Nancy? What if I hurt our newborn baby? What if I couldn't cut through the cord properly and had to clamp down on it like you do when you try to cut too many pieces of paper with a dull pair of scissors? What if—

"Mr. Patterson!" Nurse Fraulein interrupted. Shit. Had I said my thoughts out loud again? "You are going to do just fine. Please cut right here." Then she held out a three-inch section of the cord for me to cut through and smiled in the way I had seen people smile at politicians at ribbon-cutting ceremonies. So apparently, this was idiot-proof.

I made the cut.

Baby Scarlett was now officially unattached from Nancy (though not for long) and I was officially a doctor (in the same way that a person who tells a joke at a party once is a professional comedian).

While Scarlett was taken to a special area of the room, kind of like a car wash for newborns (no baby is born cute—they are a cross between a slimy alien and a greased turkey), I gave Nancy a kiss on the forehead and marvelled at what I had just seen her go through. I'm told the pain of childbirth is akin to a man wrapping his stupid bottom lip around the top of his stupid head, and after what I saw that day, I don't doubt it. Yet here was my wife, beaming from ear to ear, exhausted but somehow also remarkably energized. The moment she had been looking forward to for much, much longer than the last nine months, two weeks and twenty-seven hours was finally here. She was a mom at last. And her readiness to be a mom made me somehow ready to be a dad.

When Nancy was handed Scarlett—now much less alien turkey-like and much more "wow, she *is* cute!"—I watched them bond immediately. I guess when you carry another human being around in your womb for nine months, you gain a certain amount of familiarity. It really was surreal watching that mother and baby bond and knowing that it was my wife and my baby doing the bonding. It wasn't anything like it is in movies or on television shows, where an actress diligently tries to capture the labour process with a simulated "push, push . . . oh, look, a baby!" Then the actress is handed a child who is somewhere between a few months and nine years old and tries to act as if it is her own newborn.

Actual human mother-and-baby duos are much more like the animals you see in wildlife documentaries. The mother is ready to nourish, nurture and protect her baby at all costs. The baby, realizing which side her bread (or in this case, I guess, her breast) is buttered on, makes herself immediately the most adorable and helpless being in the universe and allows herself to be enveloped in her mother's love. Meanwhile, the father in those documentaries is often . . . not there. It's remarkable how many documentaries feature mama bears or mama leopards with no mention whatsoever of the father. What happened there? Did daddy bear say he was just going out to get some milk for the winter and then take off to a different forest? Where the hell is that deadbeat daddy leopard? Only penguin fathers seem to be present for the actual birth. And of course, male seahorses, which are the ones that actually give birth. But let's not give science any ideas here.

Fortunately, I *was* there bedside for Nancy, so she handed Scarlett to me. She did this partly so I could bond for a few moments with my newborn baby daughter and partly so she could finally eat something. (Remarkably, there is no time allotted for meals or snacks during the lengthy labour process. Which must make labour even more unfair for women who are members of a labour union.) We had packed a container of spaghetti that we were planning to share at some point. But since I hadn't wanted to eat it without Nancy, I'd slipped off to the hospital cafeteria to buy a sandwich to hold me over until after the birth. So I was sure looking forward to sharing that spaghetti . . . until I saw Nancy devouring it. Which also reminded me of a wildlife documentary, with a leopard wolfing down a yak. I thought of saying something like "Hey, I thought we were going to *split* that?!" but then

I realized that the division of labour during labour had been decidedly one-sided. So I wisely kept my mouth shut.

Back to my bonding with Scarlett.

Sure, I had aced the cutting of the cord, but anybody could do that. If you screwed up, at least the baby was still attached—if you dropped her, it was really just a fun first bungee jump. But holding the freshly un-bilicalled baby . . . well, that's something totally different. I mean, we'd been practising for this moment with fake babies in a preparation class at the hospital, but no matter how much you try to pretend an inanimate doll is your baby, you always have the reassuring knowledge that it most certainly is *not*. If you drop a fake baby, everyone laughs. If you drop your real baby . . . well, you're about to see how tough that tough woman who just went through labour for twenty-seven hours really is.

Scarlett auditions me for the job of being her dad.

So I nervously took my baby in my arms for the first time, being careful to support the head. All anyone tells you about holding a baby for the first time is "Support the head." Which, granted, is an important tip. But you also have to cradle the body. Otherwise, that sucker will slip right out of your arms because newborn babies' heads are slippery even after the weird goo is all wiped off. Write that down.

Anyway, here we were, an old but also new dad with a brand-spanking-new baby girl. (Note: We didn't spank her. That's another thing they do incorrectly in movie births. Maybe the baby actors said something saucy? I don't know. Did I mention that Nancy ate my share of the spaghetti?) After over two decades of travelling the world trying to make people laugh as a comedian and several years helping to make hundreds of thousands of radio listeners laugh at the helm of *The Debaters* on CBC Radio, I suddenly realized that it wasn't about making strangers laugh anymore. From now on, it was about helping one little girl, *our* little girl, be the happiest she could possibly be.

I remember marvelling at how small Scarlett was (Nancy might have disputed that, given her unique perspective on what had just happened). Her birth weight was eight pounds and six ounces. I mention this only because it's the first thing people ask you about your baby: "How much did she weigh!?" I don't know why people want to know this so much. Possibly because it's the only time in a woman's life you can safely ask that question.

In any case, I looked down at my beautiful eight-pound, six-ounce baby girl, who didn't even know her name yet because we hadn't told anyone and said something along the lines of "Hi Scarlett! I'm your daddy!"

"Daddy?" she said.

Well, not exactly. Scarlett couldn't speak the second she was born. She's smart, but she's not *that* smart. But I could tell by the way she was looking at me with her big brown eyes, a perfect combination of her mom's right brown eye and my left brown eye, that she knew exactly who I was. She looked right through my eyes directly into my soul, and I could hear her speak even if no one else could.

"Daddy?" she said. "You'd better not screw this up."

"I'll try my very best, little jelly bean," I whispered in her tiny ear.

Then she started wailing, perhaps already sensing that my very best might not be good enough.

So I did what every new father instinctively knows to do. I handed her back to her mom.

CHAPTER 3

Becoming Attached to Your Baby

A lot of parents say that they remember their baby's first days vividly and fondly, but I think those parents are lying. I say this because there is no time in an adult's life more exhausting than the days immediately following the birth of a child. And I say this as a DAD. For the women who actually give birth, that period is arguably even more tiring. (The "arguably" here is intended as a joke. Please, women who have given birth, don't make a voodoo doll of me and stab it repeatedly in the crotch.)

Once Scarlett had been given a clean bill of health and Nancy had held her in her arms, the transformation from euphoria to utter exhaustion began. After I quietly pledged to myself to never let anything bad happen to Scarlett, Nancy entered into a stage of sleep that was just above comatose. She looked so relaxed in her hospital bed that I thought I might have a little nap beside her. But that thought was quickly struck down by the attending nurse, who informed me that I was going to give Scarlett her first bath. I was about to say, "She's only been alive for about half an hour—how dirty can she possibly be?" but something in the nurse's eyes let me know that many a man before me had uttered this same thought and it wasn't nearly as hilarious out loud as it sounded in my head. So I just followed her and Scarlett to another room, where we went over how to gently drip warm water from a clean cloth onto her head and then repeat the process over the rest of the body. By adult standards, this wasn't a very thorough bath. Keep in mind, though, that at this point in her life, Scarlett hadn't been anywhere but the delivery room, where the hospital staff had given her the "deluxe wash" treatment straight out of the womb. So I didn't need to scrub her like I was trying to get caked-on rings off a bathtub with a Brillo pad (I don't clean bathrooms very often).

While Nancy was getting her much-needed rest, I also had the opportunity to have Scarlett go skin on skin against my chest. We had read in one of the parenting books that this helped create a bond between father and baby, and the nurses at the hospital encouraged it—provided it took place in our room and didn't result in me walking shirtless through the halls. So while Nancy slept, I reclined in the hospital chair (not technically a recliner) and held baby Scarlett firmly to my bosom (you might think dads don't have bosoms, but . . . well, I do) while she slept contentedly. That's when I realized that the feeling of your baby's skin resting on your own is the greatest feeling in the world, bar none. I can hear you pet owners saying, "I don't know—it's pretty great when little Patches puts her paws on my face and then settles down on my lap." And I'm not taking that away from you. But when mini-you rests on you with her tiny hands opening and closing for the first time, smacking her lips, oblivious to the fact that the smacking sound is coming from her, it's more than mind-blowing—it's heart-growing. Seriously, I felt what the Grinch did when he heard the Whos down in Whoville singing even after he had stolen all their Christmas presents (which is, admittedly, an arsehole move). My heart grew two sizes in that moment. Had I stolen a bunch of animated characters' Christmas presents, I would have for sure returned them right then.

From that moment on, my priorities in life officially shifted. My number-one job was to keep this little one safe and be the best dad I could be. Once she had grown up, I figured I could resume my quest to be a Major League Baseball relief pitcher. (All the practice of carrying the baby around would mean I'd probably have one arm in good shape. Which is all you really need.)

Of course, for a baby resting on a dad, the feeling of comfort and serenity is not mutual. The baby can no more control who or what she is resting on than a baseball can control where it's thrown. To the baby, you are just one in a long line of resting places or sources of heat—or most importantly, sources of food. Which is why Scarlett, upon waking on my bare chest that first time (I had fallen asleep in solidarity with mom), was immediately and rightly outraged.

She woke up nestled in the mat of my chest hair and knew that she needed food immediately then let out a scream that can best be described as a mixture of a lioness's roar and a runaway train trying to screech to a stop.

That was the first time I almost dropped her.

Not out of carelessness but out of sheer terror.

Because on your first day as a dad—or more specifically, your first nap as a dad—you may fall asleep wondering if it was all just a dream.

Is it possible that the preceding couple of days were just your sub-conscious warning you of what it *might* be like? Waking up with an infant is not a gradual process. It's the textbook definition of a rude awakening. The scream wakes you up like a blast of cold water from a fire hose, which is dangerous when the source of that fire hose is lying on your chest.

So it was that with Scarlett's scream, I shot out of the chair like a cannonball. But my new-found parental instinct, which is sort of like Spiderman's spidey senses, meant that I held on to Scarlett's head even while my own was still processing what was going on. The end result was that I somehow went from reclining in a deep sleep to standing fully awake in .001 seconds with Scarlett still on my chest. As a matter of fact, she was attached. To my nipple. The poor kid had found the right attachment for a snack, but on the wrong parent. And that's when the REAL outrage began.

I can't say for sure what was going through baby Scarlett's mind when she first bit down on my nipple, hoping for mother's milk but instead inducing a middle-aged man's shriek to harmonize with her infant's cry (imagine a duet between Barry White and Barry Gibb). I imagine the level of disappointment was what I would have felt if I'd dreamed of being in bed with a beautiful woman in sexy lingerie and woke up to find myself beside a naked Gary Busey.

And that's how Scarlett and I woke up an entire wing at St. Joseph's Health Centre that first night. She was screaming, I was screaming, Nancy woke up and she was screaming. A nurse came rushing in, and in panic mode, I pried Scarlett from my nipple and handed her off like a quarterback giving his star running back the ball for a goal line rush. The nurse calmly took the screaming football over to Nancy, and within seconds, Scarlett had latched on to one of her mother's nipples and the two began to bond in the way that only a mother and baby can. Meanwhile, I put my shirt on, rubbed my chest and said to the nurse, "Thanks. She . . . um, she bit my nipple."

The nurse nodded calmly, turned to Nancy, and said, without a hint of humour, "Good luck. You're going to need it."

CHAPTER 4

My Dad, "Slim"

The first thing you should do when you find out you're becoming a father is talk to your own father to see what advice he has to offer. In my case, that meant talking to John Chester Patterson—the man my brothers and I have always referred to as Slim.

Born in 1931 in Gaspé, a small city in Northern Quebec, Slim would eventually be the oldest of five children. He grew up in lean times (a gentle way of referring to the Great Depression) and became the man of the house at a young age because his father was away a lot (he was a military man). My dad would do whatever he could to bring in money for the household, including taking work as a delivery boy and an assistant at the local lumberyard. When his mother told him to pick up some fish for dinner, that meant going to catch something at the local watering hole. When Nancy tells me to get some fish for dinner, I go down the street to a place called Honest Weight to pay for fish that someone else has caught. And if I'm going to the local watering hole, it's to enjoy a beverage or two with a friend and not to try to provide sustenance for my family. So yes, in many ways Slim is a much more manly man than I am.

My dad never talked about his childhood very much, but I know that despite the responsibilities he had, he was also an athletic young man and a promising middle-distance runner. His times for the mile (my dad grew up long before the metric system came into use) were very competitive and he has lots of stories of old track-and-field meets where he and his teammates would jump and vault into piles of sawdust instead of landing mats. Whether this was because landing mats hadn't been invented yet or because Gaspé wanted to support its local lumber industry, I don't know. But I do know that if you're willing to vault into the air (likely with a suspect wooden pole) and land in a pile of sawdust for sport, you're either a hardcore competitive athlete or someone very, very starved for entertainment. I think my dad was a little of both.

But running was where young Slim really excelled. Literally. He would often tell me that his favourite part of running the mile was jockeying for position at the beginning of the race. In long-distance running, you don't stay in one lane like the sprinters do in their events, so it's important to get a good inside position on the track early on. This meant fighting for your territory for the first fifty yards or so. Anyone who thinks that running is a non-contact sport never ran against Slim in the late 1940s. My dad was quite proud of the fact that he'd knocked down many a competitor with his "running" skills over the years, and because running doesn't typically involve referees, he was largely unpenalized.

My dad doesn't mention it, but had he been born a few years earlier, he might well have served as an infantryman in the Second

World War. He literally dodged a bullet by barely missing the draft lottery. As it was, he and his classmates were the top of the food chain in their mid-teens and many of them were in the same position as my dad: it's time to be the man of the house, even though you're still a boy.

That's how Dad took an accelerated path to adulthood, finding a full-time job at Eaton's in 1949, when he was just eighteen years old. Shortly after that, he met my mom, Kathleen, and they had married by the time he was twenty. About nine months later, he became a dad to my oldest brother, John (at least I'm hoping it was about nine months later—but it's a little late to judge). Less than two years after that, they had my brother Larry.

So Slim was married with two children at age TWENTY-TWO!

When I was twenty-two years old, I dropped a course I was taking at university because it cut into my afternoon naptime.

You might think that being the man of the house at a young age was good fatherhood training for Slim. But he was still an athletic young man first and a father second. So when it came time to play sports in the Patterson household, my brothers didn't stand much of a chance. Whether it was football, baseball, or any sort of track event, it was going to be a full-contact contest, and Slim wasn't going to let you win. My older brothers have countless stories of being tackled during games of touch football or watching home runs sail out of the backyard as my dad took full swings at the pitches that his young sons were just learning to throw.

The first sport I remember taking part in with my dad was boxing. Not intentionally, mind you. We were outside at my brother John's house and I had assumed the pose of a boxer (I had just seen the movie *Rocky*, so I was about seven years old at the time). My dad put up his dukes to fight me, and as I took a swing with a poorly executed roundhouse, Slim instinctively countered with a perfectly timed jab that caught me right in the nose, causing my first-ever punch-induced nosebleed and delivering a valuable life lesson: learn how to fight better. Slim felt bad immediately because he was now in his late forties and had mellowed, but the experience was memorable. Slim was a scrapper, used to fighting for every inch of his life because his wife and kids depended on him—including his youngest, Stephen, whom he had just punched in the face.

Another memorable moment from Slim's young parenting days (again, before I was in the picture) involved an unfortunate incident where a driver stopped abruptly in front of him, causing my dad to slam on his brakes and my brother Mark to fly forward from the back seat and hit his head on the dashboard. (These were the days before seatbelt laws and mandatory car seats, so there was no parental neglect on Slim's part.) Once he'd checked on Mark's well-being, Dad got out of the car to have a "discussion" with the other driver, who had hit the brakes for no apparent reason. This time, the punch Slim delivered was very much intentional, and the bloody-nosed man ended up charging my dad with assault. As family legend has it, he showed up to argue the charge in a Montreal courtroom and was told by the judge that he would have to pay a twenty-dollar fine. My dad responded, "Here's another twenty. Can I hit him again?"

These stories might lead you to believe that my dad was a brute to grow up with. He wasn't. He never hit me (except for that accidental right jab). He never threatened me physically. But he did have a glare that said, "Think very carefully about what you're going to do next." Like a leopard on the prowl—only more menacing. In the *Rocky* movies, they talked about having the eye of the tiger. The band Survivor even had a hit song about it. But I'm telling you, my dad's glare would have made a tiger beg for mercy. If you're going to be a dad, you need to work on your glare game. I can't be sure, but I think my dad practised his on my older brothers so that he had perfected it by the time I came along. I'm not sure Scarlett is ready for that level of glare yet, but I still practise it on myself in the mirror almost every day. I'll keep doing it until I literally scare the crap out of myself (which will be okay because the mirror I use is in our bathroom, directly across from the toilet).

But I digress.

What I remember most about growing up with Slim was his frugality and his way with words. The first sentence I remember learning how to say is a perfect blend of these two Slim-isms. I was about five years old and I had run in the front door, leaving it wide open behind me. In my dad's mind, this meant that heat he had already paid for was escaping from the house. But rather than say, "Stephen! Close the door!" he yelled, "HEY! THE DOOR'S NOT AN ARSEHOLE—IT DOESN'T SHUT BY ITSELF!"

Poetry.

Slim's favourite word, far and away, was (and still is) "goddamn," which always made me and my brothers laugh and my very Catholic mother wince. He would say things like "Every light in the GODDAMN house is on," when just one light had been left on in the kitchen. He would say "GODDAMMIT!" when he hit himself on the thumb with a hammer, which he did a lot because he was always trying to build things rather than buy them (because everything was "TOO GODDAMN EXPENSIVE!"). And he was always cursing inanimate objects, such as a radio that had been left unplugged in the garage and exploded into sound once he'd plugged it back in with his ear flush to it, causing him to yell, "GODDAMN RADIO!"

Thinking back, Slim's approach to fatherhood was pretty much a case study of what not to say or do in front of young children. So while I don't necessarily want to model my parenting style on his, I do want to honour his work ethic. He always provided for and stood up for his family. Those are good qualities to have in a dad. And let's face it, when the person you stand up to happens to be a lot bigger than you, it doesn't hurt to be a strong long-distance runner.

John "Slim" Patterson. Legend.
(That's me and one of my brothers behind him. Without heads.)

CHAPTER 5

Find Yourself a Nancy

Despite my lack of confidence—and in fact, competence—in my first moments of being a dad, I knew that Scarlett was a lucky baby from the moment she was placed on Nancy's chest.

Sure, many think that dads are largely irrelevant in the early stages of a baby's life. After all, the mom is the source of food, comfort and safety. But who do you think keeps that food, comfort and safety source fed and safe? THIS GUY.

You may have noticed that I left out the word "comfortable" in the last paragraph.

Being a mother to a newborn *isn't* comfortable. You don't get a full night's sleep—ever. You rarely eat a full meal (I think Nancy's last full meal to this day was the spaghetti she wolfed down at the hospital) and your body has been repurposed to provide nourishment to another human being. Yes, I'm talking about breastfeeding and, yes,

I will talk about it a LOT more a little later. But for now, let's focus on Nancy.

We met in Montreal in 2009, when she was serving as an event coordinator for Sarah's Fund. This is an organization devoted to making life as comfortable as possible for children going through cancer treatments. Nancy took the job largely because she had lost her own mother to cancer when she was three years old, and also because she had met Sarah Cook, the inspiration for the fund, and immediately wanted to help out in any way she could.

The job was demanding and required organizational skills, patience and a lot of kowtowing to wealthy prospective donors. It's the kind of job I wouldn't have lasted in for more than a day (of course, I wouldn't last a day in a *lot* of jobs). But Nancy thrived in that environment and she kept her focus on the greater goal of raising money for children with cancer rather than the immediate challenge of dealing with wealthy arseholes.

At this point, you're probably wondering, "So how did YOU meet her, Steve? You're not . . . wealthy."

True. But one of the perks of being a comedian is that you often find yourself at functions you would never have been invited to if you weren't funny. Also, these functions are often for legitimately good causes, so it's bearable and even sometimes enjoyable to entertain at these events, where you get to meet some truly inspiring people (mixed in with the arseholes).

I had been hired through the comedy festival Just for Laughs (thanks again to JFL CEO Bruce Hills for booking me that night!) to do a show for the Sarah's Fund golf tournament, entertaining a room full of doctors and wealthy businesspeople. It was the kind of function I had performed at a number of times before (and hope to do many more times in the future). I researched the people who would be there, prepared material just for them and hoped to God they would enjoy it. If people like that enjoy your show, there's a good chance someone in the group will hire you to do another, or you'll get invited to come back in following years. I certainly didn't head into this function with the goal of finding a wife and the future mother of my children, but that's what happened. So I guess the lesson here is to aim higher!

While I'd like to say that sparks flew between Nancy and me immediately, or that it was love at first sight (I would actually never like to say either of those things), in reality, our relationship started less as a shock of lightning and more as a storm cloud that led to thunder, then an angry storm, then silence, and then, eventually, a mixture of sun and cloud.

This analogy is even confusing me—and I wrote it. So I'll try to explain more clearly.

I liked Nancy the moment I saw her, partly because she's a beautiful woman, and partly because the first words she said to me were "Hi, can I get you a drink?" It turned out that she was just doing her job, but I didn't know that at the time, and unlike many people who attend posh events, I don't expect people to offer me drinks the second I meet them.

I can't remember exactly how I responded, but it would have been pretty off-brand of me to refuse a drink, so I'm sure I was happily seated with said beverage a few minutes later. I remember thinking, "Wow, that's a pretty woman," which was interesting because (1) I had a girlfriend at the time (more on that in a bit), and (2) Nancy had a baseball cap pulled down over her face, since she was circulating around the golf course seeing to the high-maintenance needs of the high rollers in attendance.

After I finished my comedy set (which went as well as could be expected in that kind of setting—meaning people listened and laughed at the right times and some of the CEOs occasionally glanced up from their cellphones), I spoke with Nancy quite a bit and we made plans to attend a hockey game courtesy of one of the main donors to the charity, Montreal Canadiens legend Bob Gainey!

We had a great time at the game, and even though there was no talk of it being a "date"—with nary a holding of the hand or a kiss goodnight—it did have a certain date-like quality to it. Then the next morning, I was doing a radio interview with a local Montreal station about another show I had coming up, and the hosts asked about the "hot Frenchwoman" I had moved to Montreal to be with—referring to my girlfriend at the time, whom I had neglected to mention to Nancy.

Nance was angry. Maybe the angriest she's ever been with me—which, as any man who has been married for a number of years knows, is saying something. She phoned me up specifically to tell me that she might not ever speak to me again. For some men, this is more of a tempting offer than a threat. (I'm KIDDING, Nance. Love you!)

In retrospect, I suppose I should have mentioned that I had a girlfriend. But here's the thing: Nancy also had a *boyfriend*, and she hadn't mentioned him to *me*.

So after that first non-date, we didn't speak for quite a while. I think it was almost a year before we had both ended our relationships and I invited her on our first official date, to the celebrated Montreal restaurant Joe Beef, which, as you may have guessed by the name, is worshipped mostly by carnivores. We sat at one of the better tables in the small restaurant and shared a magnificent meal of beef, oysters and wine. The date went so fantastically that . . . well, it never really ended.

Nancy moved into my Montreal condominium not long after that and I knew for sure that it was true love when I went to buy her underwear one day. It was either that or try to wash the ones she already had at my place without wrecking them, which is a skill I still haven't mastered. (Honestly, there are "delicates" and then there are "don't even try, buddy.") If, as a man, you find yourself shopping for women's underwear, I truly believe you have found "the one." Or else you have a serious fetish, which I don't want to be judgy about, but they just don't look comfortable for a man to wear.

In my case, I had found "the one."

We got married on April 29, 2011, in St. Lucia, choosing a Friday because we were sure no one else would get married on that day of the week. As it turned out, quite a few other couples had the same idea—including two people who took a little of the focus away from us: Prince William and Kate Middleton.

But Nancy didn't panic when we found out we were sharing a date with a royal wedding (even though we picked it first). In fact, we made a joke out of it and thought of issuing commemorative plates and other ridiculous memorabilia just for the fun of it. (It turns out that's a pretty expensive joke.) This was my first indication that I had chosen the perfect "go with the flow" bride.

The second was that Nancy didn't stop smiling for a second, even though it poured rain the entire week of our wedding in what was supposed to be the Caribbean dry season. She smiled when a bridge washed out and the limousine that was supposed to take her to the church couldn't meet her, leaving her in a decidedly less luxurious cab. And when that same storm wiped out the outdoor wedding reception we had planned and forced us to bring a steel drum band indoors. (Steel drums are generally—and correctly—considered to be outdoor instruments. Their volume is roughly akin to the noise of a jet taking off while playing a jaunty all-steel version of "Killing Me Softly." Which is ironic.) Through it all, Nancy held her beautiful smile and when we went outside into the cloud-filled Caribbean sky, *she* picked *me* up for a photo! Some men would be emasculated by this, but I'm hoping she can piggyback me around full time once I reach my sixties.

Not long after we were married, Nancy and I made the move to Toronto from Montreal. It was a move back home for me and away from home for Nance, but I felt there were more comedy opportunities (English-language ones, anyway) in Toronto, and Nancy was excited at the prospect of a new start. It's one of the many things I love about her: her ability to adapt to change and uncertainty. This skill is important in comedy *and* in parenting. She also gave up her job as an event coordinator for a non-profit organization to become my manager in Canadian comedy, which is *not* a non-profit organization. At least not intentionally.

Having your spouse as your business manager doesn't work for everyone. For one thing, the same person is telling you what to do at home and at work. Also, it's difficult to confide in your spouse about times when your boss is being an arsehole. But as we come up on a decade of living and working this way, I can honestly say that Nancy is somehow both the best manager and the best mom I've ever seen in action. Around our house she is the momager, which can make for some weird hybrid conversations:

"Can you change Scarlett's diaper, and did you bring the receipts home from your trip to Vancouver?"

"Um, I don't know."

"You don't know how to change a diaper?"

"No, I don't know if I brought those receipts home."

Eye-roll followed by exasperated sigh.

But this is also a great way to ensure that your manager is working in your best interests. Not that I think other managers are ripping off their comedians—though some for SURE are—but when you can keep commissions in the household and late-night conversations in bed with your manager aren't considered a conflict of interest, it makes for a healthier work relationship.

Sure, there are challenges to working with your spouse while simultaneously raising a child. Like how to decipher those work–family conversations, or when to schedule actual work meetings and actual family time. I admit that I'm not great when it comes to time management, and sometimes my job cuts significantly into family time (including, ironically, writing a book about being a dad while simultaneously being a dad). But I can't think of anyone I would rather be in the foxhole of parenting with than Nancy. She takes on every challenge that being a momager brings—including being married to a professional smartass—with all she's got.

I won't say she makes being a dad easy because it's not an easy job—nor should it be. (If you find it easy, you need to start trying harder.) But she makes it at least possible for me to be a good dad who really wants to improve. Nancy's amazing and far-reaching abilities as a mom include but are not limited to:

- arts and crafts
- baking (especially birthday cakes)
- decorating
- swimming instruction
- Ukrainian Easter egg making (I know it's an art and a craft, but honestly, given the amount of time it takes, it deserves its own mention—plus it's cool that she knows this when she has zero Ukrainian background)

I knew Nancy was going to be a great mom even *before* she became a mom based on how much she cared for others, how patient she was in times when I would not be (that is, most times) and how much children were drawn to her. She jokes that her high-pitched voice makes children think she's one of them, and in fairness, there might be something to that. But more importantly, she just gives off an aura of caring.

I remember being at the zoo in Toronto's High Park with her not long after we moved to town and before Scarlett had come along. Out of nowhere, a little girl about four or five years old came up to her, took hold of her hand and said, "Mommy?" Nancy patiently looked around for the girl's actual mother, who was nearby and looked a *lot* more like the girl than Nancy did (the little girl happened to be Black), but to the child, Nancy just seemed like a good person who could help her find her mom, which she did within a few minutes.

Kids are great judges of character, much like dogs. That's why kids and dogs usually get along so well. When we adults hear a dog's bark or a baby's monosyllabic "DA!" we often think they're just making sure we know they're there, but I'm convinced they're warning each other that somewhere nearby is an adult who is an arsehole. So if you're ever alone in a room with a baby and a dog and they both start making loud noises for no apparent reason, you can be sure they're discussing how much of an arsehole you are. So don't yell at them to stop when this happens. Apologize and get them both a snack immediately. On the other hand, if a dog or a baby smiles happily at you, you can rest assured that you're a good person (or at least you've just given them a good snack).

Nancy is beloved by kids and dogs and me. She is the most genuinely kind and honest person I've ever met. She is the exact kind of mom you would want to raise children with. But guess what? *You* can't. Because she's raising *mine* with me. So back off!

But I do sincerely hope you find or have found a Nancy of your own.

Pretty clear which one of us more than carries her own weight in parenting and in life.
(Photo credit: John Hryniuk.)

CHAPTER 6

When It's Difficult to Conceive

It's a cruel twist of nature when women who would be some of the best moms in the world have difficulty getting or staying pregnant.

Before we were blessed with Scarlett, Nancy and I had several miscarriages. I say it this way because while it was Nancy who bore the terrible brunt of physical pain and loss, I shared the emotional pain with her. I knew how much she wanted to become a mom and how much she had made me want to become a dad.

It was only after discussing our miscarriages with friends that I learned how many of them had also had similar experiences. People just don't talk about it. There is a stigma associated with losing a baby. It's as if you somehow weren't doing everything within your power, every step of the way, to ensure a healthy pregnancy. People think you just get married and then, a few months later, announce you're pregnant. But it doesn't always work that way. So the worst thing you can possibly ask a recently married couple is if they're pregnant, and if not, why? If you find yourself thinking of doing this as a joke—trust me, don't.

Our quest to have a child was made additionally stressful by the fact that my wife is a professional planner. When you plan events for a living, there is no event more worth planning than your own pregnancy! So Nancy came to me with an ovulation schedule that let me know her prime time for conception. This was the time when, not unlike a hired horse stud, I would need to be ready to fulfill my duty.

We began trying to conceive right after we were married . . . well, not *right* after. It would have been disrespectful to start right there in the church, in front of our family and friends. Plus the tuxedo was a rental, so I couldn't risk the extra cleaning charge. But we did begin trying while on our honeymoon in St. Lucia. While we were basking in both the Caribbean sun and the newlywed glow, we tried multiple times to make a baby. Please note that this is different than making love. At least it was for me. When we were trying to make a baby, all I could think about was "Let's make a baby." When we were making love, all I could think about was baseball statistics. (If I have to explain this to you, you're a better lover than I am, so congratulations.)

Despite our best efforts, we returned from our honeymoon and passed through the weeks and months that followed without any "we're expecting" news for all the ladies in our family who were eagerly anticipating it. Despite Nancy's well-organized and well-advertised ovulation schedule (she would post her dates on our household calendar the way most people post their upcoming vacations), we were having trouble getting pregnant. So everybody's well-meaning questions became points of agitation and stress:

"When are you going to have kids?"

"Whenever the time is right, I guess."

"So . . . soon, you think?"

"I don't know. When are *you* going to stop being such a nosy arsehole? Now, pass the potatoes, please, Grandma."

I'm paraphrasing slightly (I never asked my grandma to pass the potatoes), but that is how agitated we were feeling.

I can't think of a more intrusive question to ask a woman than when she is planning to have children. Except maybe asking a woman who you *think* is pregnant when she's due. Better to err on the side of caution until you see what is for *sure* a baby bump. And even then, let someone else verify it first:

"Oh, look at you! When are you expecting?"

"Expecting what?"

"Oh . . . um, your tax return. I got mine by direct deposit last week."

"Really? But it's November."

"Yes. Well, I have a different year-end . . ."

I was forty years old when Nancy and I got married (she was thirty-two, if you're wondering), and while men certainly can have children later in life, there is a definite decrease in the potency factor from younger days. Not to be too crude about it, but if it takes a million sperm to find and fertilize one egg, you'd better save them up for when it really counts.

Happily and eventually (I couldn't tell you exactly how long, but I'm sure Nancy has it down to the minute), we were able to get pregnant. Then came the real challenge of making sure that the pregnancy progressed properly.

Nancy did everything right. She increased her iron and folic acid intake, changed her eating and drinking habits (she stopped drinking alcohol entirely—just one more reason it's a good thing that the procreative fate of the world isn't in the hands of me and my buddies), but still she suffered a miscarriage. Then another. Then another. Each time, Nancy's heart was broken and mine along with it. The pain I felt seeing her dream of motherhood fading was as much as I could take. I can't imagine what she was going through.

When the first miscarriage happened, we took a break, regrouped and tried again. The second time, we did the same. But after the third, I started to doubt whether we should or could go through the whole process again on our own, so we decided to go to a fertility clinic. It was a very professional place and our doctor was apparently so good at her job that she was pregnant herself, which I suppose was the greatest endorsement of their work.

The fertility clinic was where the act of making a baby became all about science. It came complete with a support group that wasn't quite in the room with us at the time but might as well have been. And by "support group," I don't mean a team of people cheering you on, calling out from the sidelines with helpful encouragement like "Attaboy, Steve! Get right in there!" That would have been horrible. What I mean is that Nancy's ovulation cycle, which she had already been tracking carefully herself, was now being monitored by a team of medical professionals. They were able to pinpoint not just the prime day, but the prime hours, minutes and, if I'm being honest, prime seconds for optimal conception—which, let's face it, sounds like a weird character from the *Transformers*.

We scrupulously followed the fertility clinic's advice, which included specific vitamins for Nancy and lifestyle changes for me. In particular, I had to reduce my weekly alcohol intake from whatever number it was to something drastically less. I also had to bring my marijuana intake down to zero, since apparently "happy smoke" makes sperm very unhappy (that had never come up in conversation with my marijuana-smoking friends).

Don't get me wrong—I wasn't an alcoholic stoner by any stretch of the imagination. But I'm a beer drinker and have been since (insert "legal drinking age" here), and when you're a professional comedian, there are also ample opportunities to share the odd toke here and there. Plus, both alcohol and marijuana are now officially legal in Canada, so I'm not a felon. But if you're a man trying to get your partner pregnant, put down the bong, buddy. There's not going to be any bong time after the baby comes anyway, so you might as well get used to it.

Marijuana is terrible for your sperm's motility—which is like "mobility," but with an extra *t* and one less *b*. Actually, motility is a measurement of your sperm's forward progression. Basically, if your sperm aren't moving forward fast enough, they'll never make it to the egg. Sort of like a baseball player who has to run fast enough to make it to home plate before he's thrown out. (I told you I think about baseball during sex.) Meanwhile, because I needed to be ready at literally a moment's notice, I was given a prescription for Cialis, which I didn't feel I needed. If you're a man pondering using these pills, I won't try to talk you out of it. But I will say that you should take them *only* if sexual activity with your partner is imminent. Otherwise . . . well, let's just say you're going to have to cancel that casual stroll around the block if you ever want to look your neighbours in the eye again. But on the bright side, if there's a limbo contest going on at the time, you can serve as the bar!

Nancy had downloaded a handy app to her phone and we would receive a call from the clinic when it was optimal conception time.

I can't begin to express how odd it was to get a call from a stranger, even a medical professional, telling us it was time to have sex. What made it even creepier was that it was a robotic automated message. It was like going to an ATM and having it tell you to strip out of your clothes and get busy. This led to what is certainly the most awkward moment a man can have with his brother-in-law.

I can hear you saying, "What?" Just keep reading.

Long story short, Nancy would get the calls and the automated message—or Robopimp, as I began to refer to her (the only way it could have been more awkward is if it had sounded like my mother's voice)—would tell us it was time to get busy. I'd have to get in the mood immediately. Which I suppose is easy for men in their late teens or early twenties, but when you're in your early forties, it takes a little time. Especially when it's the middle of the afternoon and you were just watching a story on *Dr. Phil* about why men in their forties need to work out longer to get the results they used to in their thirties. This was depressing to me for a couple of reasons: (1) because I hate when things take longer than they used to, and (2) I didn't really work out in my thirties.

Plus, being told that it's time for your penis to magically begin to produce another human life, like some sort of magic wand that wouldn't be allowed within five football fields of Hogwarts, is a lot of pressure. Not to mention, when you *know* that you're having sex for the express purpose of reproduction, you are essentially trying to do what your parents did when they had you. And if that visual comes into your mind . . . well, there's no pill in the world that can get you up for the task.

In any case, we had gone through this weird version of phone sex a couple of times already: Robopimp would call (hopefully I was home when the call came in—otherwise, I'd have to rush back from wherever I was) and I'd pop my just-in-case pill and hope for the best. Then Nancy and I would look at each other, try to summon up instant sexy poses, and usually end up laughing while we fell into bed and indeed "got busy." Afterwards, Nancy would lie on her back with her legs in the air because she had heard that an elevated position might help the sperm find their mark. Meanwhile, I would sit beside her trying to think of encouraging things to say, like "I really felt like one of those sperms was the one!" or "Take *that*, egg!

It was an awkward time.

However, it was never more awkward than when another call came in right after we got Robopimp's message—which, if you're wondering, sounded exactly like a telemarketer's pre-recorded pitch to get you to hire a duct-cleaning company: "Hi! You have reached your optimal conception time. And you can now receive up to 30 percent off on cleaning out your ducts!"

Nancy and I had a familiar ritual for getting in the mood—it involved brushing our teeth, a little personal grooming and then a race to the bedroom. Of course, I also had the option of popping a Cialis to speed things along, which I had just done on this particular occasion. I knew it would take about twenty minutes for that to kick in, so in the meantime . . . well, I just had to make sure I wasn't standing too close to any shelves of glassware or pottery.

Then Nancy's phone rang again. This time, it was her brother Paul, who lived in Florida but was near Toronto for work and had called to say he was on his way over for a rare visit. As a matter of fact, as Paul put it, "I'm just down the road!"

Now, I'm not sure if I've mentioned this yet, but Nancy is the most honest person in the world. Especially with her family. So while another person—maybe *any* other person—would have asked her brother to delay his visit for just a few minutes and left it at that, Nancy told him exactly WHY we needed him to delay.

"Oh, you're that close?" she said. "Well, we just got a call from the fertility clinic and we have to have sex. Can you go to the pub on the corner for a bit and then Steve will come meet you when we're done?"

Paul was silent on the other end of the phone. But not as silent as I was sitting beside Nancy, even though my jaw had dropped and my mouth was wide open.

"Uh . . . yeah, sure," Paul said, then immediately hung up.

I asked the question that any husband in the same situation would have asked: "WHAT THE HELL DID YOU SAY *THAT* FOR?"

"What? He knows we're trying. It's no big deal."

"No big *deal*? Your brother now has the visual of his sister having sex and then the guy from that visual is going to meet him for a *beer*? How is that *not* a big deal, Nancy?"

And so began the most awkward session of intercourse in my sexual history—or perhaps sexual history in general. So many thoughts entered my mind: What would I say to Paul, who was waiting for me at that pub down the street? Was he thinking about his sister having sex with me? Would this Cialis-induced erection ever go back down, or should I call a doctor?

"You won't need to call a doctor, Steve. Now *focus*!" Nancy said from the missionary position. Apparently, I had been thinking out loud again.

So I focused. I concentrated. I sent my little soldiers on their mission (is *that* why it's called the missionary position?). Then I prepared to go and meet my brother-in-law.

As I was shaking my head and pulling my pants on, Nancy asked me what was wrong.

"I just feel like this is going to be an awkward meeting with your brother, that's all."

"Do you want me to call him and tell him we're done and you're on your way?"

"No, thank you. I don't think that will make it less awkward."

Then I walked to the corner pub with a sweater around my waist despite the sweltering summer heat. I found Paul, ordered a beer and we sat in silence while we drank. And we've never spoken about that afternoon since.

What makes this all even weirder is that despite all the science and vitamins and lifestyle changes, this particular session still did not lead to a baby. So essentially, I had kept Paul waiting so I could have casual sex with his sister.

It remains the only thing more awkward than getting a booty call from Robopimp.

CHAPTER 7

Riderville

In late 2013, after two years of trying to become pregnant and three heartbreaking miscarriages, an arsenal of strategic vitamins, regular calls from Robopimp and the most awkward beer-drinking session that two brothers-in-law could ever have, we decided to take a break from trying to have a baby. This is not to say we took a vow of celibacy or agreed that we wouldn't ever try again. We just decided not to focus on it. No visits to the clinic. No deposits from me into an unfortunate plastic cup for analysis. (I purposefully left this part out before. You're welcome.) Instead, we would just enjoy each other's company.

This meant that Nancy could come with me that November to the Grey Cup (Canada's Super Bowl!) in Regina, Saskatchewan, where I was booked to do a show for the Saskatchewan Roughriders. The Roughriders—or Riders, as most of their fans call them—are the Canadian Football League team with the most faithful and fanatical fan base. I had performed for the team once before, during Grey Cup luncheon festivities in Toronto in 2012, and had foolishly booked a voice-over audio audition later in the day. The luncheon show went well. The voice audition afterwards did not. It turns out that partaking in the hospitality of the Riders fan base is an all-day commitment. This is because you will be offered a *lot* of Canadian-style Pilsner, a beer that Prairie residents (especially those in Saskatchewan and eastern Alberta) feel a personal responsibility to consume on every occasion possible.

I had a lot of fun entertaining that group. Then I drank a lot of Pilsner. Then I went to a voice audition in downtown Toronto.

I honestly can't remember what the audition was for, but clearly it wasn't for "man drunk on Pilsner beer" or I most definitely would have nailed my performance. Instead, I showed up decked out in the green-and-white colours of the Saskatchewan Roughriders, with a bunch of beads hanging around my neck, my face painted with the Riders' logo on each cheek and a pair of oversized novelty sunglasses with flashing LED lights covering my eyes. I looked like I had just come from either New Orleans Mardi Gras or a debauched New Year's Eve party. In short, I stood out from the other voice actors in the room, who all looked . . . well, very normal by comparison.

I took a seat in the studio waiting room, the lights of my glasses still flashing, and tried to strike up a conversation with some of the other actors. But no one wanted to talk to me. Fair enough. I looked like a wayward Saskatchewan man who had wandered into the big city, lost all his friends and stumbled into a recording studio.

"Ah, sir? Can I help you?" the flummoxed and fearful receptionist asked.

"Yeah, I'm here for da oddishion," I replied.

"Okay. For [insert name of product here—I honestly can't remember]?"

"Yeah, datssit," I slurred.

"What's your name?" she said.

"Stave Pattershun," I proudly and loudly proclaimed.

"Oh, you're Steve Patterson? I love *The Debaters*!" she exclaimed, changing her tone completely. Which is also when the other actors in the room, some of whom I knew, perked up.

"Steve! How are you? Where the hell did you just come from?"

"RIDERVILLE!" I yelled.

Then we all cheered. Then I went in and did the worst voice audition I have ever done, probably destroying the microphone with Pilsner fumes in the process. And then I headed *back* to the Riderville party. Those were my people.

Fast-forward to 2013—the Riders had booked me for another luncheon show (mostly because I'd gone back to their party and told them the story of my failed voice audition), but this time we were IN Saskatchewan and the Riders were IN the Grey Cup!

If you haven't been to a Grey Cup weekend in Canada, you are missing one of the best annual parties the country has to offer. Fans of all the teams in the league (sure, there are only nine teams, but it's still nice that they all show up) come to whichever city is hosting the game and take over the town for that weekend. Or at least, they take over the smaller western cities. The celebration can get lost in the shuffle in cities like Toronto, Montreal and Vancouver. But on the prairies, Grey Cup week takes over everything. And in Regina in 2013, with the Roughriders in the Grey Cup and heavily favoured to win over the Hamilton Tiger-Cats, it was *the* most joyful party in North America. Period.

Even Martin Short and Tom Hanks showed up. Mr. Short because he grew up in Hamilton and is a legitimate Tiger-Cats fan, and Mr. Hanks because he is, by all accounts, a legitimately kind man. So when his good friend Marty said, "Hey, you wanna come watch a football game in rural Canada in minus-thirty-degree weather?" Hanks probably said something like "Sure! Life is a box of chocolates!" Even if those chocolates freeze up while you sit watching a game you don't know the rules of, while being constantly hounded for selfies and autographs by people in Skidoo suits.

During the game, Nancy and I actually ended up sitting near Marty and Tom (it's been a paragraph now, so we're on a first-name basis), but we didn't bother them—partly because I've never been one to hound celebrities for autographs and partly because we hadn't dressed properly for the game and might have been frozen to the metal seats. Also, Tom Hanks seemed like small potatoes compared to a *real* Canadian celebrity—someone I happened to know personally and had spent a large portion of the previous two nights with: comedian, actor and *Corner Gas* creator Brent Butt.

Now, to say that Brent is a huge Canadian comedy success story is a major understatement. For years, he had been known on the West Coast and by comedians all across Canada as one of the country's funniest people. His style of delivery is distinctly small town, but his material draws on situations that anyone with a good sense of humour can relate to. It took the rest of the country a while to catch up, but when Brent's *Corner Gas*, a sitcom set in a gas station in rural Saskatchewan, finally caught on, it was a massive, unprecedented success. This catapulted him to household-name status across Canada, and especially in Saskatchewan, where he's from. Brent would have been at the Grey Cup to cheer on his beloved Roughriders regardless of whether the league had invited him to perform. But he was slated to perform, and the rest of the time he could be found in the epicentre of the party: Riderville.

Now, as I've already pointed out, Riderville is a great party in any city that's hosting the Grey Cup. But Riderville IN Regina, during a Grey Cup the Riders were playing in? It wasn't merely a party—it was a religious experience. And the only thing that could make Riderville, in Saskatchewan, with the Riders IN the Grey Cup, even more divine was to be there drinking Pilsner with Brent Butt!

I'm not sure what the most apt analogy would be. At the Playboy Mansion with Hugh Hefner (if Hugh Hefner and the Playmates were all middle-aged men and women wearing Riders jerseys)? At a Democratic convention with Barack and Michelle Obama? At the second-to-last supper with Jesus Christ? Point is, Brent Butt is like a magnet in a pin factory. Only the pins are deliriously star-struck Canadians presenting complimentary Pilsner beers.

Also, Riderville in Regina was a massive event. In Toronto, the Grey Cup had taken over a couple of hotel ballrooms. In Saskatchewan, it was in a giant complex of several buildings, the largest of which was usually used for either livestock auctions or political events (which, when you think about it, are pretty similar: both are trying to sell you something that stinks).

Brent and I met up after our respective shows. I introduced him to Nancy (his wife, like a surprising number of comedians' wives, is also named Nancy—proof that Nancies have refined senses of humour) and we were given a corner table near the bar in the back of the large showroom to take in the festivities and swap comedy stories. (New show idea: *Corner Table*?) Now, I don't know how many other professions do this, but when comedians run into each other in a crowded public setting and they're friendly (i.e., non-arsehole types), they will hang out together. There's really no better play-by-play partner for people-watching than a quick-witted comedian. And there is literally no better person to have beers with in Riderville than Brent Butt.

But while we were watching people, people were watching Brent.

Saskatchewanians lined up to buy Brent beers and talk to him. Sometimes they wanted to talk about *Corner Gas*. But more often, they wanted to talk about their relatives who knew his relatives. This is the reality of Canadian celebrity in a nutshell.

People didn't even waste time saying, "Hey, you're Brent Butt!" They just walked up, shook his hand and said things like "My cousin worked with your uncle on a farm in Tisdale in 1986." (That is, verbatim, what one person said.) Brent would respond with a cheerful "Oh yeah? Well, that checks out!" Then they would pose for photos and the person would hand Brent a Pilsner. He would then pass many of those beers to me and we proceeded to get quite pleasantly drunk. Or at least I did. Brent might have been sober the whole time. He's a very good actor.

Brent was gracious about introducing me to people, and a few did recognize me from various TV comedy specials I'd done. But this was his backyard, and a hit sitcom makes you more recognizable to people than a few TV specials and a national radio show. Not that I'm complaining. I quite like not being recognized. Especially when I'm in the midst of trying to set a new record for free Pilsners consumed in a condensed period of time.

Nancy also loved the party. She wasn't partaking in the Pilsners, but she was laughing happily along at people's stories, moving to live music from top-notch Canadian bands like the Barenaked Ladies and the Sheepdogs, and getting to know Brent. All you really need to know about him is that he is a humble, hard-working Canadian comedian who did the rarest of all things: became famous while staying in Canada! There is less of that in this country than there are Sasquatch sightings. True story.

Anyway, you're probably wondering where I'm going with all this. Is this a book about parenting or drinking with Brent Butt? Well, I'm telling you all this because this story leads directly to Scarlett's conception. Which now is conjuring up weird mental images of Brent Butt. That wasn't my intention! I'm just trying to tell the whole story here.

The point is, surrounded by fun-loving football revellers, grooving to some great music and basking in the glory of hanging out with the Prairie version of Jesus Christ, Nancy and I were the most relaxed we'd been in months. Later that night, we were just enjoying being with each other, nestled in a cozy hotel room when the weather outside was frightful. So inside we got pure . . . delightful. And the rest, as they say, is a baby.

I can't say for sure when it happened. We spent a lot of time in the hotel room when I wasn't performing comedy or revelling in Riderville. I can't imagine it happened after we attended the football game, though. (The Riders soundly trounced the Tiger-Cats, by the way. So I guarantee that Scarlett isn't the only child who was conceived in Regina that weekend.) All I can say is that without the pressure of trying to conceive, the mathematical precision of scheduling "optimal conceiving sessions," the stress of wanting not to disappoint Nancy, and the desperate feeling that this had to be the time, it finally *was* the time.

Now, does this mean that if you're trying to conceive a baby, you should find a party with thousands of Saskatchewan Roughrider fans, seek out Brent Butt and pound back a whole bunch of Pilsners? No. I don't think Brent offers his services as a baby conception whisperer, and there's a reason Pilsner was not on the list of recommended supplements at the fertility clinic.

But when it comes to the journey of conception, which is ridiculously easy for some and devastatingly difficult for others, you sometimes just have to get out of your own head. I truly believe there is an element of trying too hard. You put pressure on yourself to perform. You create mental stress, which in turn creates all sorts of physical challenges. But a living being coming from another living being, while certainly scientifically explainable, has an element of the miraculous. As much as we can help that miracle along, we can also sometimes get in our own way.

So to those who desperately want to have a baby and are pursuing various methods to make it happen, I wish you the absolute best. I encourage you to do all the research you can and to use different fertility methods when the natural method isn't working for you. But first, do try to do what comes naturally. Give yourselves a chance to just be yourselves. Make sure that you're not trying too hard to be natural. This is much easier said than done when you're in the midst of trying to conceive, but sometimes when you and your spouse really want to bring a baby into the world, you simply need to focus on each other.

That or I can just give you Brent's contact information and see if he'll meet you for a few Pilsners.

CHAPTER 8

Changing Diapers

If you ask any new parent, and certainly any new dad, for his or her least favourite/most gross parental chore, the answer undoubtedly will be changing diapers. If you meet a parent who says anything different, that person is either a liar or perhaps a dung scientist. Otherwise, there is nothing in the world that can prepare you for what lies beneath. And I say this as the parent who has probably changed only 1/1000 of the diapers in the family. But that first time was enough to leave a lasting impression that no amount of counselling will ever erase.

For those who have never had to change a baby's diaper . . . well, you win this round. And yes, the joys of parenting, the sound of your child's laughter and the smell of a freshly bathed baby are wonders that I wouldn't trade for anything. EXCEPT for not having to change a diaper. If all the good baby sights and smells came without that most vile excursion into indecent scents, it would be a perfect existence. This is why many parents opt to hire a nanny or caregiver to do all that dirty work while they swoop in to take the plum parenting duties, like walking the freshly changed baby in a stroller or even bet-ter showing off the sleeping baby (that someone else managed to get to sleep).

The problem is that you don't know exactly when your baby is going to dirty his or her diaper. So if you really don't want to deal with that, you'll need the professional diaper-changer on hand at all times—and that is an awfully expensive way to tell your children, "You'll be my number-one priority one day, but not for a while." Or I guess you could just allow the baby to ramble around commando, soiling whatever is underneath her. But this is supposed to be what separates the humans from the rest of the animal kingdom.

Obviously I don't remember my mom changing my diaper (maybe I was one of those commando kids?), but since I was the youngest of five sons, she must have really had that task down by the time it got around to me. Which, from what I'm told, is tougher with little boys than with little girls because . . . well, little boys have a little hose to spray you with. And from what I know of boys (having once been one), I'm convinced that when that happens, they do it on purpose.

My main challenge in having a girl baby, if I'm honest, was learn-ing about the female anatomy in a whole new way. Having never had a vagina, I really wasn't sure about the maintenance of that area. Men have trouble enough satisfying their lady's private area, but when it comes to being a dad of a baby girl, it's time to rethink things com-pletely. As in, not think about it at all. Clean quickly but carefully, then get the hell out of there!

Baby boy or baby girl, you're going to need to change a lot of diapers, because babies go through them like young Hollywood celebrities go through significant others. The only difference is that diapers don't have their publicists issue a statement when they've been completely soiled and are in desperate need of a change.

Hence, here are the five steps to changing a baby's diaper for amateur diaper-changers. I will list these in roman numerals because once you have successfully changed a diaper, you have indeed secured a *V* for victory.

I. Confirm That the Diaper Needs Changing

This will become apparent rather quickly through the obvious olfactory indicator. Every baby is beautifully unique, complex and different. But the smell of a soiled diaper—that is universal. It's as if a farmer has mistaken your child for his field and dumped concentrated manure into the diaper in the hopes it will grow into something lucrative, nutritious and delicious. (Note: It most definitely will NOT.) The smell doesn't sneak up on you like a tiptoeing burglar—it bursts in proudly, causing the people in the room (usually just the two parents, since everyone else is out somewhere having fun) to look at each other in an accusatory manner.

"Oh God, Steve! Was that you?" I remember Nancy saying the first time Scarlett woke herself—and us—up with her little gift.

"No, it wasn't me!" I replied indignantly (while also making a mental note that the next time it *was* me and Scarlett was in the room, I would totally blame her). "It must have been Scarlett!"

For some reason, though, my wife didn't believe me. So Nancy picked up Scarlett and put her nose so close up to our baby's butt, the poor kid must have felt like a drug mule foiled by an airport canine. Then Nance took an audible whiff, as if she were judging a tulip festival.

"Oh God!" she said through a coughing fit and watering eyes.

"I told you it was her," I exclaimed proudly. I was being brave only because I knew my wife was too exhausted to slap me.

II. The Unwrapping

No matter how many diapers you change, you will always be in denial that something so vile could come from your adorable, perfect descendant. The first time I opened one of Scarlett's diapers, I expected to see solid little pellets, like a rabbit sometimes leaves in your garden or like the ones domesticated bunnies leave at the bottom of cages. But instead, Scarlett's poop (and I imagine the poop of other babies also, though I don't care to verify) looked like something a volcano might have spewed out. The colour can't be described (though I did once see someone driving a BMW inexplicably painted that colour). It's more green than brown, but it's also very dark—not surprisingly, rather like evil volcanic ash, since it has come from hell. It's also astounding how much odour the magical material from which diapers are made actually contains. Because the waft that awaits you when you unwrap this devil's dowry is a cross between the world's most rotten onion and the best variety of AXE body spray. If you haven't experienced AXE before, take it from me—it's not a pleasant smell. It's a cross between insect repellant and . . . well, any other repulsive smell you can think of. Yet it is marketed to young men as being appealing to young women. Presumably young women with no sense of smell. In any case, soiled diapers smell almost as bad as AXE body spray, so when you confront the aroma for the first time, you will soon be crying as uncontrollably as your baby is. If you can, this is a good time to find some gloves that you won't have to wear ever again.

All the while, you are trying to maintain some semblance of being the adult in charge of the situation.

Of course, baby Scarlett didn't know this. To her, I was just a blubbering giant blocking his nose and screaming, "Oh my God! Oh God! This is disgusting!" Any female will tell you that this is not an acceptable way to address a lady.

III. The Wiping

So now Scarlett was scream-crying and I was scream-crying right along with her. The double dose of despair woke up Nancy, who—and I still don't know *how* she did this—calmly took the diaper out from under Scarlett, disposed of it in the Diaper Genie (an ingenious device that takes soiled diapers and somehow contains the scent so that your entire house doesn't smell like the inside of a thousand dirty diapers), quickly wiped the source of the demonic eruption, applied some soothing cream to the area and then put on a new diaper—all seemingly in one motion. This immediately calmed Scarlett down and supplanted her outraged cries for help with an expression that said, "Ahhhhhhhh, finally there's an adult in charge."

Nancy gave me a quick look as if to say, "Thanks for trying." I took several of Scarlett's wipes to use on my hands (which hadn't even seen active duty), on my tear-streaked face and finally on my forehead, hoping they could wipe away the memory of what I had just experienced.

Naturally, I became more experienced in subsequent diaper changes and eventually I grew into what I would call an adequate diaper-changer. Not an expert, of course. (I've heard there are parents out there who can literally change a diaper in their sleep. Which is extremely handy, since that's when diapers seem to need changing the most.) But at least I do know enough to follow the golden rule of wiping a baby girl: FRONT TO BACK. You don't wipe the other way because then there's a risk of getting volcano evil baby vomit into your little girl's vagina, and that is exactly as disgusting as it sounds. This technique made total sense once it was explained to me, but it had never been explained to me before. My brothers and I had, of course, never discussed it and it's also not something you really talk about with your buddies who are dads to girls. "Hey, Ted, helluva shot there. Was that a seven iron? Say, how do you properly wipe your daughter's vagina?"

So front to back is the way to go.

But you have to actually give the area a wipe too. It's just difficult finding the right amount of pressure for the cleaning. Your touch should be lighter than when you're trying to scrub a pot clean after you burned the pasta, but not so light that you don't make contact. This was something I had difficulty understanding at first. The last thing I wanted to do was hurt my daughter in any way. Especially in any way that affected the most female of her body parts. So when I was wiping her, I was really giving more of a fake wipe. Like something a mime would do with an imaginary cloth. And this wasn't helping poor Scarlett because babies *need* a proper wipe or else things get infected.

After some coaxing and correcting from Nancy, I finally learned the proper technique to get Scarlett sufficiently clean. Still, whenever she needed a wipe throughout infancy and toddlerhood, it was pretty clear who she preferred the wiper to be. Which was fine with me because . . . well, frankly, this was not the job I was looking to be the go-to parent for.

Also, Nancy and I differed on the number of baby wipes to use each time. She was efficient enough to use only one on most occasions, no matter how disgusting the eruption, while I was much more of a "use however many we have left" kind of guy.

IV. The Wiping . . . with a Twist

In their chapters on diaper changing, parenting guides don't tell you that just when you think you've mastered the deed, your baby will come up with a twist on things. Literally. She will refuse to be on her back for any length of time and will turn over and attempt to crawl away just as you're trying to fasten the diaper. It's not unlike a salmon on dry land desperately trying to get back into the river. This is something that's impossible to mimic on fake "practice babies," or even on real-life newborns before they develop the ability to be free-range. If you really want to know what it's like to change a baby's diaper, go to a rodeo and try to wrestle a small calf.

And yet, diaper changing is something that Nancy knew innately how to do. She was able to pin Scarlett down (gently) with one hand while expertly attaching the diaper with the other. For me, it was a full-on battle, pleading with Scarlett to stop flipping. "Come on, Scarlett! Stay down!" I would yell, like a boxing trainer who doesn't want his fighter to get up off the canvas. She would respond with a loud cry, which, loosely translated, was "Noooooooooo! I've got a lot of fight left in me, Dad. Come on, round two!" I know it amused Nancy to see this battle going on, as evidenced by the fact that she often laughed and wouldn't help me. But I persevered. I wanted to be a competent dad. And competent dads change diapers. Period.

V. Zippers, Not Snaps!

Once the offending evil diaper has been cleared and the new one (which has no idea what it's in for) has been securely wrestled into place, all you need to do is put the baby's pyjamas back on. Unless, of course, you dress the baby in clothes other than pyjamas. You should know, however, that if you do that, you're wasting your time.

Babyhood is the one time in your life when wearing pyjamas outside of your own home is not only acceptable but expected. Babies in pyjamas are cute, even when sporting the inevitable bit of drool as an accessory. Go out in public with a baby in pyjamas, a bit of drool dripping down her face, and people will say, "Awwww! She's so cute!" Meanwhile, I puked on my shirt at a wedding once and everyone was all "You're GROSS, Steve!" In retrospect, it wasn't the ideal behaviour for a best man.

But getting back to the pyjamas, when you're buying some for your baby, get the ones with the zipper! Not the snaps! Snaps are impossible to fasten because they never line up properly and you'll always end up starting again, which your baby will not have the patience for. Zippers, ironically, do up in a snap.

All that said, there is one great thing about changing diapers: it generally means your baby will have her bare belly exposed at some point. And when that happens, it's zerbert time. Which, in case it's not universally known, is the art of pressing your lips against your baby's belly, pursing them together like you're playing a tuba, and then blowing out air. This will cause a noise not unlike the sound of a long, wet fart—with the important difference that it is *not* a long, wet fart. If done properly, the zerbert will cause your baby to laugh uncontrollably and that will cause you to laugh uncontrollably right along with her. It will also help you forget about the struggle you just went through to get the fresh diaper on. So in a way, it's similar to childbirth! It's gross when you're in the middle of it, but the end result is a happy, sweet-smelling baby! (Note: This is sarcasm. In no way is a dad changing a diaper like a mom giving birth. You should *not* try this joke on your wife unless you want to wake up one morning with a soiled diaper as a sleep mask.)

CHAPTER 9

It Doesn't Go By So Fast

Babies bring incredible highlights into your life: their smiles, their first movements and sounds, their first laughs. (FYI, making your baby laugh is a better feeling than making a theatre full of people laugh. True story.) But honestly, the best moments you'll have as a new parent are the times when your baby is asleep.

A lot of parents won't admit this. They talk about how much fun it is to be with their little bundle of joy and about all the glorious moments of discovery. In fact, the phrase parents commonly use to describe this time is "it goes by so fast." Well, I have news for you: it doesn't. A night with a teething, irritated baby goes by slower than a snail piggybacking on a sloth across a Velcro-covered highway, and makes for an impossibly long next day. And I'm saying this as a parent who travels a lot for work and, even when he is home, doesn't have a traditional day job to wake up for the next morning.

You know when time goes by fast? When you're sleeping, that's when. Sleep is your own personal time machine.

Think about it. You drift off to sleep and enter into dreamland; where you go in your dreams is up to you. For me, it's usually back to my high school days, where I'm running around as the quarterback of our football team, throwing the winning touchdown pass for the state championship! This is an especially strange dream for me because:

1. My high school didn't have a football team.
2. If it had had a football team, there's no way I would have been the starting quarterback.
3. I went to high school in London, Ontario, so even if the team had existed, it wouldn't have been eligible for a state championship.

But that's the great thing about dreams—they take you wherever you want to go. Even places that don't exist. Until you are awakened by a place that very much *does* exist: your house with a newborn baby who will, under *no* circumstances, sleep through the night.

To all the dads out there who get up for nighttime feedings, whether to give a bottle to the baby or just offer moral support to your wife—you are good men. But not quite heroes. Heroes are the moms who can wake up from a dead sleep that they just collapsed into moments before and immediately take the living, screaming alarm clock from the crib to their bosom in a way that is 1,000 percent more gentle than when people slam the snooze button or throw their cellphones across the room to silence the wake-up notification (BTW don't do this with your baby).

I was truly in awe of Nancy whenever I saw her arise from her much-needed sleep to tend to Scarlett's screams. My wife had never reacted that way to me when I woke up in the middle of the night crying for a sandwich.

Yet for all the damage that sleep deprivation does to a person (refer to a more scientific book if you want to know the specifics—I just know that it makes you put dishes back in weird places and think you have answered questions out loud when you haven't even moved your lips), there is a strange bonding experience that happens when parents go through it together. So much so, in fact, that I actually felt bad when I missed out on missing out on sleep.

I'll explain.

A month after Scarlett was born, I had to do a month-long comedy tour starting in Western Canada. This meant that I would be several thousand kilometres and three time zones away while Nancy was facing the daunting task of parenting on her own. She certainly had the tougher job of the two of us (though in fairness to me, that one show in Duncan, British Columbia, was no picnic), but it was emotionally the most difficult tour I have ever done. Partly because I missed being at home and "helping" with the baby (not that Scarlett even noticed I wasn't there), but mostly because I actually felt guilty for the sleep I was getting.

Yes, it's a lot easier to think, "Gee, I shouldn't be getting all this sleep," as you fall asleep in a comfortable, quiet hotel room than it is to actually not get sleep. But the guilt of getting sleep while your spouse is not is a real thing. Still, it's certainly not the same as having a tiny human suckle from you like a vampire. I was winning the battle of sleep but losing the time at home with my newborn baby girl.

Ever since people started having babies, this is the bargain that has been struck by parents who have to travel for extended periods of time. You're on the road trying to provide for your family, but you wish you were at home with your family. It's like trying to have your cake and eat it too, but much more challenging because . . . well, whenever I have cake, I eat it. Pretty straightforward, really.

During the month I was on the road and Scarlett was at home with Nancy, we were fortunate to have Nancy's stepmother, Debra (who is a strong candidate for best mother-in-law in the world—and I'm not just saying that because she'll likely read this book), stay with us. I know that grandmas, nanas, or in our case, nonnas have been doing this for many generations, but seriously, if we hadn't had our nonna in that first month, I might have had to abandon the tour. Not because I thought Nancy couldn't handle it, but because I couldn't deal with the guilt.

I'm really thankful we had the help then. We don't have any immediate family members in our city, and while I suppose we could have paid for a nanny, Nancy and I had decided from the beginning that we would raise our child ourselves. This is definitely more challenging and exhausting than having outside help, but the upside is that our baby will know who her parents are and not wonder why the lady who doesn't really look like her is around more often than the one who does.

I also learned that when you miss a month in a newborn's life, you miss a *lot*.

Scarlett had an issue with her tongue when she was born. Basically, her tongue was tied, a condition called ankyloglossia (which, ironically, is a bit of a tongue-twister when you try to say it). This restricted the range of movement of her tongue, causing her a lot of physical pain whenever she tried to eat (which was basically whenever she was awake). So Nancy and Nonna took her to a specialist who somehow untied her tongue, making the whole situation much better. When Nancy explained on a phone call later that day how much pain little Scarlett had gone through during the procedure, I was both heartbroken and happy that I'd missed it. Heartbroken that I wasn't there to comfort Nancy and Scarlett, and happy because I really didn't want to see my baby girl in pain.

Nevertheless, the procedure was a great success. Afterwards, Scarlett fed more happily, which meant she was happier in general, which meant she went to sleep more easily, which meant Nancy could get a little sleep, which meant I didn't feel as bad getting more sleep on the road. A classic win-win-win-win-win situation.

Nancy, Scarlett and Nonna settled into a good routine while I was gone, eating, sleeping, smiling and laughing. (They say babies can't technically laugh at first. But Scarlett could. Genetics, I guess.) By the time I was ready to head back home, with twenty or so shows under my belt and lots of adults left laughing, my main job was to let Nancy get some rest by helping to put the baby to sleep.

It was a tough transition to make.

First of all, baby bedtime is much, much earlier than adult comedy showtime. The schedule I had become used to on the road was to start my day at around 4 p.m. with some exercise, a light bite to eat and a review of the evening's material, followed by the show and ending with a late dinner.

Not surprisingly, babies don't follow that kind of schedule.

My exercise time was Scarlett's naptime. My light bite to eat was even lighter because babies are remarkably needy meal companions and often insist on being held while you are eating, which rules out knife-and-fork meal options. My "ramping up energy" time was Scarlett's naptime. And while I'm never averse to a good nap, it's tough to teach your body a new rhythm. Even as I write this sentence, I'm aware that there is a helluva lot more rhythm change going on for the moms. They basically have to be ready to conga at all times with an overly aggressive dance partner attached to them. For a dad used to performing at night, it's more a question of bottling up energy so as not to confuse sleeptime for playtime. That's a rookie move that is okay to make if you're a young uncle and can eventually leave. But it's not okay at all if you're an old dad.

I remember storming into Scarlett's room one time, in the same way I would take to the stage to start a comedy show, and being met with a baby's startled screams and a mother's stone-cold death stare. That stare would have made a ruthless military general apologize meekly and back out of the room. I only did that once. I never want to see that look again.

But even worse was the first time I remember trying to get Scarlett to sleep by myself. I tried softly rocking in the chair, then gently bouncing her while walking around the room singing altogether inappropriate songs. (My go-to song was "We've Got Tonight" by Bob Seger. He said he wrote the song about a love scene in the movie *The Sting* and summed up the encounter between two world-weary strangers as follows: "I'm tired. It's late at night. I know you don't really dig me, and I don't really dig you, but this is all we've got, so let's do it." That's not a song a father should sing to his newborn daughter. But the beginning of the song is "I know it's late. I know you're weary," and the melody is relaxing, so it's a little confusing.)

Scarlett proves that she wears hats better than me.

Truth be told, during the first week or two back off the road with a newborn, all that guilt I had been feeling for getting more sleep than Nancy while I was away was quickly replaced by the phenomenon known as baby brain, which takes hold of all new moms and all dads who at least try to take on some of the newborn nocturnal duties.

We had a co-sleeper device for Scarlett that allowed her to—wait for it—co-sleep with us in the bed. This might be the best creation for newborn babies since babies themselves, or maybe the Diaper Genie. But basically, it's a bassinet that fits in the middle of the bed, with netting on each side that allows babies to sleep with their parents without the danger of being squashed by the mother or (much more likely) the snoring, oblivious father. The main benefit, though, of the co-sleeper is to allow mothers to breastfeed without getting out of bed. And Nancy had this nighttime routine so down pat that she could at times feed Scarlett WHILE SLEEPING. When she heard Scarlett whimper, she would automatically pull the baby out of the co-sleeper, feed her and put her back in. At least I'm told that's what happened. I was sleeping at the time.

I do remember a couple of times I was in bed with Scarlett without a co-sleeper and was completely paranoid that I would roll over her. I didn't sleep at all those nights. There was also the time that I dreamed Scarlett had crawled over me and was falling off the bed, so I dove head first onto our hardwood floor, landing with a thud, which then woke Scarlett, who had been sleeping comfortably in the bed the whole time.

I'm pretty sure that's one of Nancy's favourite fathering moments of mine.

Mostly, though, Nancy and I had different tactics for getting baby Scarlett to sleep and we have maintained those tactics as she has grown into toddlerhood. Nancy will sing, cuddle, coddle, rock, roll, read or do anything else to ease Scarlett into sleep. I, on the other hand, am much more of a lead-by-example type of guy. So I prefer to fall asleep first, sometimes less than one full page into a children's book (usually just enough time for one rhyming couplet) and hope that Scarlett will follow soon after.

But neither of us subscribes to the "let them cry it out" school of getting babies to sleep. I know it's a thing that many parents do. I'm sure if it had been up to my dad, my brothers and I would have cried ourselves to sleep every night. But Nancy and I believe that a baby who falls asleep knowing her parents are there for her is a happier baby than one who eventually passes out, completely exhausted, thinking her parents have abandoned her.

Quote all the studies you want, but I believe this "cry it out" method sets a dangerous precedent that most parenting books won't tell you about. If you're ever walking, hiking or skiing with those same babies once they've grown up to be adults, and you fall, cry out in pain and are in need of assistance, their subconscious might kick in with crib flashbacks. Then they will leave you alone to fend for yourself, possibly to be found by wild dogs three days later (which is about how long some nights with your newborn will feel as you try to comfort her to sleep).

You will get through it—I promise. But as you're going through it, you will rightly think to yourself, "This doesn't seem to be going by so fast right now." Well, guess what? It isn't. So at least you have the satisfaction that you're correct about that.

CHAPTER 10

How I Became a "Dadvocate" for Breastfeeding

Studies vary on exactly what and how much children should eat, but I find that experts everywhere agree children should, in fact, eat something every day.

In infancy, this starts with mother's milk—or formula, for those who aren't able to breastfeed. Exactly what goes into that "formula," I'm not really sure. But I hope it's not the same stuff that goes into Vicks Formula 44 cough syrup, because that stuff tastes awful. Take it from me: baby formula tastes better. It's not important how I know this.

In our case, we were fortunate that Nancy was able to breastfeed. Well, more specifically, *Scarlett* was fortunate. Because breastfeeding creates a bond between mother and baby roughly akin to the one shared by a man and his TV remote. I know most adults don't like to think back to when they were suckling at their mother's breasts (if you do, you should seek professional counselling), but there really is nothing like breast milk for nutrition, convenience, and let's be completely honest, the desexualization of the boobies. (Note: If it were more widely known as "boobie-feeding," maybe people wouldn't get so uptight when it happens in public.) What were once looked upon as twin peaks of titillation suddenly transform into a baby's all-u-can-burp buffet, which might as well come with a "No Dads Allowed" sign.

This is not to say that new moms aren't beautiful. They are. ESPECIALLY NANCY. She was the most beautiful new mom I've ever seen. I mean IS. She IS the most beautiful . . . er, let's move on. New moms have a glow that no amount of sleep deprivation can dim. And breastfeeding is the most natural form of food delivery in the world, which is why so many mammals do it. Basically, every mother with a nipple (and most have more than one) will breastfeed her young because it is nature's divine design. But also because animals in the wild can't be bothered carrying around and sterilizing bottles of baby formula. Heck, baby giraffes suckle while standing and walking, and the mother giraffes don't even break stride! *That* is efficiency. Yet you don't hear of other animals coming over and asking them to cover up or "go do that somewhere else."

Why?

Well, partly because animals use human words only in movies and cartoons. But more importantly, society has taught us that a woman's breasts are items of sexual attraction. (Note: Men's breasts have never caught on in quite the same way—at least not those of the men who seem to be the first to go shirtless in warmer weather.) When a woman has large, accentuated breasts, there are many among us, men and women alike, who might think, "Wow! Those are nice breasts!" (Try very hard not to say this thought out loud if you have a tendency to do such things.)

I get it. I've been there (before I was married to Nancy, of course). Now if I see a woman with large, accentuated breasts, I glance at my watch, say, "Look at the time—I gotta go!" and then run away. But once you've seen your beloved little baby suckling from your beloved spouse's breasts, it's much less "Wow, look at those!" and much more "This is perfectly natural, but I'm going to look somewhere else immediately."

Before I became a dad, I didn't feel this way.

Which I should probably explain.

This doesn't mean that when I was a young man and saw a woman breastfeeding her baby in public, I would pull up a chair, grab a bag of popcorn and settle in for the full session. There is such a thing as being *too* into breastfeeding, especially if it involves a complete stranger. But I wasn't comfortable with the concept of breastfeeding in public. I felt, for no good reason, that breastfeeding was something that should always be done at home.

It's only after you become a parent that you realize sometimes babies need to eat while they're out with their moms. And yes, moms of newborns do need to get out of the house sometimes, because they spend all their time when they're in the house keeping another human being ALIVE. Sometimes they need a change of scenery. If anything, there should be designated public times when *only* breast-feeding moms are allowed in public spaces. So please be respectful of new moms who want to take a walk or simply sit down on a chair other than the one they are rocking in for hours every day.

Usually, a mom who is nursing her baby in public will wear a purpose-made breastfeeding top while draping herself in a blanket for some privacy. But in some cases, this isn't possible (usually because the baby is throwing the blanket off its face because that's not a terribly comfortable way to eat). This can cause the breast (aka boobie) to become more exposed. This is where things get difficult for young men. If you are in your late teens to early twenties and spot any form of exposed breast, it will likely be the highlight of your young life and you will find it impossible to tear your eyes away. To those young men, I offer this piece of advice: pretend the boobie with the baby attached (which somehow hasn't desexualized it for you) is your mother's. There. That ought to do it.

A woman who is breastfeeding in public is doing so because her baby is screaming in hunger and/or her breasts are screaming in pain. I remember Nancy telling me that she knew when Scarlett was hungry because her boobs hurt. You can't be much more connected with another human's rhythms than that. It's like a superhero sonar.

Wife: "You there! Husband. Go get the baby!"

Husband: "Why? What's wrong?"

Wife: "She's hungry."

Husband: "How do you know?"

Wife: "Because my boobs hurt, that's how! Get the baby right now before I shoot this milk out at you!"

Husband: "AAAAAHHHHHH!" (Runs to get baby.)

There is very little that gets a new dad moving faster than the prospect of imminent lactation. I learned not to question this process after a while. It really doesn't seem fair, though. The woman had to go through the excruciating pain of childbirth and now, every time that baby is hungry, she must feel pain *again*? For the sake of equality, it should be that whenever the baby is hungry, his or her dad feels a firm flick to the groin (not hard enough to take him down, but just enough to remind him "You're a dad now and it's feeding time"). I realize that Nancy would be more than happy to include this step in the feeding-time ritual, so I'm hoping she doesn't read this part of the book.

All of this to say, when you see a new mom discreetly breastfeeding in public, you should give her and the baby some space and get on with your life. It's really quite simple. Yet for some reason, many people, especially in North America, seem to think that mothers shouldn't breastfeed their babies in public at all because it is too "disturbing."

If it sounds like I have a specific example in mind, it's because I do.

When Scarlett was a little over three months old, we took her to an NFL game in Tampa Bay, Florida. I know a lot of parents wouldn't do this, but keep in mind that parents of newborns are people too. They deserve to be out at events, just like non-parents of newborns. If anything, they deserve to be out *more*. Plus, the trip had been orchestrated brilliantly by my brother-in-law Paul, who had convinced his young daughter, Scarlett's cousin Lila, that a trip across Florida, from their home near West Palm Beach to Tampa Bay, to see a football game would be a nice way to celebrate her seventh birthday. Also, the game included my favourite team, the New Orleans Saints. So really, it was like it was my birthday. But of course, Lila had some specific demands, as any soon-to-be seven-year-old should.

What were those demands? Well, she agreed that we could all go to the game together, in an RV that Paul had rented. But on the way, we would have to attend a rodeo and celebrate her birthday with a theme based on Disney's hit movie *Frozen*.

So it was that we found ourselves at a real live Florida rodeo, where I gleefully acted slightly inappropriately at every possible turn and then explained to anyone who would listen, "Sorry, it's my first rodeo." (It's important to do jokes to amuse yourself sometimes.) After that, we rolled into the massive parking lot beside the stadium in Tampa Bay to take part in pre-game tailgating festivities. Now, if you thought that tailgating was just a lot of people drinking beer, barbecuing meat, eating said meat and playing a game called cornhole (which involves throwing small sacks of resin into holes that have been drilled into wooden ramps) . . . well, you'd be absolutely correct.

Soon, thousands of people had shown up in the parking lot with the colours of their team adorning their vehicles: black and gold for New Orleans, deep orange and pewter for Tampa. And right there with them was our group in the light blue and ice colours of the movie *Frozen*. Sure, we got some weird looks, but ultimately even rough-and-tough American football fans are not immune to the charms of little girls dressed up as princesses singing the song "Let It Go" (at least not the first few times through). Plus, as if I didn't love my Saints enough going into the game, I learned that day that their fans are revered around the league for their culinary skills when it comes to barbecue. Many showed up in vehicles towing smokers that had been lovingly smoking meat for hours on end (in some cases, even from the night before), filling the air with the smell of Cajun shrimp, brisket and jambalaya.

Once the Saints fans found out that I was also a Saints fan (not hard to do, since we were all adorned in Saints jerseys, including little Scarlett), they got over the fact that we appeared to be cheering on princesses from a fictitious land named Arendelle and offered us some of their incredible food, which I devoured like a ravenous hyena (part of growing up as the youngest and smallest of five sons). Also, I learned something that day I would really come to appreciate throughout Scarlett's baby and then toddler years: when you are a baby or are with a baby, people give you stuff. All the time. Sure, it's often candy, which you have to politely refuse, since (1) you should never take candy from strangers, and (2) babies don't even have teeth. But sometimes it's delectable Cajun brisket. And there's a good reason that the expression "Don't take Cajun brisket from strangers" doesn't exist. Because Cajun brisket is GODDAMN DELICIOUS!

In any case, the trip to Tampa had pretty much paid for itself before the game even started. By that point, we had consumed literally a truckload of food, tossed a lot of resin sacks through a lot of holes and downed enough beer to ensure that we wouldn't have to consume any more at twelve dollars a can (American!) inside the stadium. Then we took our seats, high up in the stands, where the Florida sunshine could beat down on us with such strength that it felt as though we were being barbecued ourselves. This obviously wasn't the best environment for an infant, but I will point out that we had brought a good pair of noise-cancelling headphones and enough sunscreen to survive a week on the surface of the actual sun without the hint of a tan, let alone a burn (Scarlett inherited my Irish complexion, poor kid).

Honestly, we were having a great day. Until it was time for Nancy to breastfeed. We went down to the concourse level, where she draped a blanket over herself and began to feed Scarlett while I acted like a human shield to make things even more discreet. But that wasn't enough. In short order, we were approached by a stadium staff member, a young man who looked to be in his late teens. He came over and said, in a cracking voice, "Um, you can't do that here." Nancy opened her mouth to respond, but this was a job for me as her husband. So I replied—calmly, I thought—"What the hell are you talking about, kid?" He then proceeded to explain that the stadium had a strict no-breastfeeding policy and said there was a room under the stands where Nancy would have to go.

She removed her nipple from Scarlett's mouth. The baby reacted the exact same way I would have if someone had removed a cheese-burger from my mouth while I was eating it: she screamed bloody murder. Suddenly, our discreet feeding wasn't discreet anymore. Purely because of an idiotic policy being carried out by a clueless teenager.

I felt bad for the stadium kid, actually. But not as bad as I felt for my own daughter and wife. So I explained to him—again calmly, I thought—"You've made my baby cry and my wife upset. So I suggest you go get a manager who is an adult."

A few minutes later, the teenager returned with his manager. He was a large man who appeared to be in his thirties and had likely not listed "stadium security manager" as the dream job on his bucket list. He carried that chip on his shoulder like a pirate carries a parrot. (It was perfect that he worked for the Tampa Bay Buccaneers.)

"Sir, your wife can't do that here," he barked.

"Why not?" I barked back.

Nancy could see things escalating, and since she is as opposed to physical confrontation as I am all for it, she tensed up, which in turn made Scarlett start to cry again.

"It is stadium policy. We have a room you can go to for that."

"We don't need a room—" I began angrily. But Nancy cut me off.

"It's okay, Steve. We'll go to this room."

So we followed security manager Biff (I'm not sure that was his name, but it easily *could* have been) and his teenage sidekick, Chip (he could have fit on Biff's shoulder), to the breastfeeding room under the stands. It could best be described as a slightly less appealing

Guantanamo Bay. It had a single light bulb, no furniture except for a metal chair and no air circulation whatsoever. Which was just as well because the air that was trapped inside smelled like it had been there since Mary tried to breastfeed Jesus and was asked to leave the stable by one of the Three Wise Men.

Nancy took one look (and one whiff) and said, "No, thanks."

Biff said, "Why not?"

And Nancy replied, "Would YOU want to eat in here?" Then she walked away.

I was very proud of her at that moment. It was a good line to walk out on—even if, judging by his physique, Biff would eat anything, anywhere, at any time.

I waited until Nancy couldn't hear me, then I turned to Biff and Chip and said, "You know, you've got a bunch of guys without shirts on at the game today whose breasts are truly disgusting to see. You should put THEM in here to eat." Then I walked away too.

Not a bad line, but not as good as Nancy's.

When we got back to our seats, Nancy continued to feed Scarlett under her blanket, while I told the rest of our crew what had happened. Everyone was immediately angry. The Americans in our group in fact suggested we sue the stadium, the city of Tampa Bay and perhaps even the National Football League. I understand that in America, litigation is a legitimate response to everything from a breach of human rights to a slight disagreement over a game of cornhole. But we're really not the litigious types. Plus, the National Football League, which openly ignored the effects of concussions on players for decades and would adorn cheerleaders in dental floss if allowed, probably isn't too concerned with progressive policies. Especially when it comes to women.

It's really just common sense to allow human beings to engage in the most natural form of nourishment known, provided, of course, that the mother isn't shooting the breast milk at others like a water pistol (an urge I fully admit I would not be able to resist if I could lactate—which is probably why God didn't give men that option) and also that the child being breastfed is, in fact, an infant. Otherwise, this policy could really go awry after a particularly festive pre-game tailgating session. This is an insight I never would have had before becoming a dad and it's why I'm now a full "dadvocate" of breastfeeding in public.

By the way, when we got back to our seats at the game, Nancy, still angered, exclaimed, "Look at those cheerleaders! They're showing more cleavage than I was when I was feeding Scarlett!"

To which I instantly replied, "Look at the time—I gotta go!" and then ran away.

CHAPTER 11

"I Don't Mind"

The first time I realized that Scarlett is smarter than me was when she was four years old.

Sure, there had been mounting evidence before that. Like the many times she accessed features on my cellphone that I never knew existed. Or the ease with which she learned to swim in a few short lessons while I'm still trying to figure it out well into my forties. But the moment that really drove home Scarlett's mental superiority was when I saw four-year-old her carrying a chair down the stairs at our house.

I said to her, firmly but not yelling, "Scarlett! That chair is too big to carry down the stairs. Stop, please!"

And she replied, calmly, "I don't mind."

It's a statement that might at first seem apathetic. But the more I thought about it, the more I realized that it was quite empowering.

At the very least, if your father tells you not to carry something down the stairs, and you, a four-year-old girl, respond, "I don't mind," you will have temporarily paralyzed him with confusion.

He will stop to wonder, "Did I ask her if she would 'mind' not carrying the chair? Or did I specifically tell her *not* to do it?"

And while the dad is pondering this, the little girl will simply continue to walk down said stairs, with said chair, even stopping briefly to say, "Move, please, Daddy," at which point her father, still confused, will step aside.

Now, experts may tell you that children who talk back to their parents should be disciplined or at the very least given a time out. I agree that kids need to be guided as to what is right and what is wrong. But yelling at a child whenever she utters an independent thought, or striking a child, ever, is abusive and frankly moronic behaviour. Parenting takes patience and resilience. Mostly, though, it requires remembering what it was like to *be* a child.

For most adults, this seems to be difficult. Perhaps this is because most adults have jobs that require them not to act like children. For instance, if your accountant suddenly has a tantrum in a meeting with you because he is tired of adding up numbers, you will most likely hire a new accountant. Or if you go to your doctor complaining of chest pains and she wraps a *PAW Patrol* bandage around your finger and says, "There, that ought to fix it!" you should find out at the very least where that doctor went to medical school.

Young children are just figuring things out. Their brains are still developing, so correcting behaviour without telling them why it's wrong is . . . well, wrong.

We've all seen parents gently (and sometimes not so gently)

correcting their kids in public. The vast majority of parents I've seen do it with patience and encouragement:

"No, we're not getting a toy for you because we came in to get a toy for your friend's birthday. Put that back, please."

The child gets bummed and protests: "But I *need* a toy."

Then the parent takes it up a notch: "You do not *need* a toy. You *want* a toy."

Then the child uses the parent's logic against him or her (if it's actually logical, it's usually her): "Fine! I WANT a toy, then!" Thrust and parry.

Then the parent shows the child who is boss: "I understand you want that toy. But that's not what we came in to buy today. And you can't always get what you want." (A surprising amount of good parenting advice has been given by Mick Jagger.)

Then the child's lip starts to quiver and you know the tears can't be far behind. But the wise parent pre-empts those tears with "And if you start to cry, we have to go home instead of to the party. Is that what you want?" Then the tear tsunami is seemingly miraculously stopped in its tracks. This is because children (1) always want to go to parties, (2) understand what's at stake better than most adults, and (3) can, despite what people think, control their crying like master puppeteers (or in this case, I guess, "puppe-tears").

Then the parent gives the child a kiss on the forehead and they continue shopping.

Contrast that scenario with a child who says to a parent, "BUY ME THIS!" Then the parent responds, "NO!" and the child screams, "WHY NOT!?" Then the parent cuffs the kid on the head and says, "THAT'S WHY!"

That's not parenting—that's bullying.

So what do you do when your child responds to a direct order not to carry a chair down the stairs with the phrase "I don't mind"?

Well, I would suggest picking up that child before she falls down the stairs and getting the chair out of her hands, and then, once you're both safely off the stairs, you can pre-empt her protest by saying, "And do you MIND that there is a tickle monster on the loose in the house right now?" And once you've playfully chased your child around the level flooring of your home, gotten in a few good tickles and replaced the cries of indignation with laughter, you can explain why it's unsafe to walk down the stairs holding a chair: "Because then you might get badly hurt, and that would make us both very sad. And I don't like being sad, do you?"

And if you're very lucky and have been very patient, your sweet child will look up at you and say, with equal compassion and understanding, "No, Daddy. I don't like being sad."

Then she'll give you a kiss on the cheek, pick up the chair, and head back towards the stairs. Apparently, when it comes to my sadness . . . well, she just doesn't mind.

CHAPTER 12

The Arsehole Desk

The problem—and perhaps danger—in trying to recall life lessons that your dad taught you as a kid is that you may find you can't think of many specific examples.

To be perfectly honest, most of the lessons my dad passed on to me had to do with frugality and character and simply not being an arsehole.

When he wasn't yelling things that would have gotten younger me into trouble for repeating, Slim was building things from wood in a decidedly non-traditional woodworking sort of way.

I can remember when Dad built a desk for the bedroom that my older brother Ross and I shared. It would have been easier to buy a new desk at Canadian Tire or just have Ross do his homework at the kitchen table (which Slim had also built). As a matter of fact, our house was filled with wooden things my dad had built. There were wooden hooks for pots and pans in the kitchen, but many homes wouldn't have needed because they would have had cupboards for storage. (But who in their right mind would build wooden cupboards. Idiots!) Instead, Slim created large wooden hooks that were glued to an even larger wooden hook holder. These hooks then held our pots, our pans and an assortment of ladles and forks—many of which featured wooden handles that Slim had also crafted himself. Basically, anything that could have and *should* have been made out of materials other than wood, Slim would try to make himself. But why? Why all of the wood projects throughout our home? Well, I guess he just had a passion for woodworking and loved craftsmanship and the challenge of . . . actually, no. It was because Slim worked for a lumber company at the time, so he got the wood for free.

Anyway, back to the desk.

I remember the wood was dark—much darker than pine or oak. It was more like the bark of a tree, rather than the lumber that's found beneath. This was not so much a design choice, of course, but more about what wood was available for free at the lumberyard that day. I also remember we didn't have much margin for error, since the quantity of wood we had would barely allow for a desk high enough to sit under, even for me. (I was seven years old at the time. Ross was thirteen and already the size of a full-grown man. So I knew in my heart this desk was really for me.) Dad followed the old woodworker's rule of "measure twice, cut once," and I remember that he was quite proud as he cut four uniform pieces of the mysterious dark wood without wrecking anything (otherwise, our desk would have had three legs).

From there, it was a simple matter of gluing a few pieces of wood together to form the top of the desk and then attaching the aforementioned legs. If you're wondering where the drawer would go, the answer is on another desk, I guess. There simply wasn't enough wood for a drawer. And besides, as Slim so eloquently put it, "Who needs a goddamn drawer on a goddamn desk? Just keep everything where you can see it!"

Fair enough.

Through the construction process, Ross and I were responsible for keeping everything balanced and staying out of Slim's light as he focused on drilling, hammering, or (my favourite) sawing. It was always thrilling to serve as Slim's apprentice on sawing projects because after he started up his power saw, his apprentice (me) would hold on for dear life to the object being sawed. (This wasn't always wood. I distinctly remember him trying to saw through metal shower door tracks and at least one steel pipe.) And always he would let you know (deadly power saw in hand) that you had to "stay out of the goddamn light" so he could see the line he was sawing. It was a high-stakes assistant's job because, technically, if he kept sawing "in the dark," he would not only risk making a crooked cut but could also dismember you. This became a risk he was willing to take more and more with each subsequent son. And again, I was the last of five.

Fortunately, the sawing part of this particular project was already done.

Now Ross and I were doing our best to hold the heavy and heavily suspect homemade desktop steady while Slim prepared to attach the equally suspect wooden legs. We had the desktop positioned over the four legs and were doing our best to keep everything upright when Dad began hammering (he had decided to both glue and nail the desk together so that it would, in fact, outlive us all). I remember that Ross asked if it would be a better idea to use screws to attach the legs to which Slim replied with something along the lines of "I don't have enough screws—nails will be fine." I have since learned that this is not, in fact, the best way to decide which of those two fasteners to use.

But eventually, Slim had three out of the four legs nailed into place and was looking pretty proud of himself. He was admiring his handiwork as he hammered in the last nail and he started to say, "This is going to be the best goddamn desk that—OUCH!! MON DIEU COL EN DU BIEN!" (Slim sometimes swore in French thinking we wouldn't understand what he was saying. He was right.) He had completely missed the nail he was hammering, but not his thumbnail. In retaliation, he slammed his fist down on the desktop, which hurt him but not the desk. So he slammed it a second time, and that *did* hurt the desk. Since the desktop was just suspect wood glued together with, as it turns out, suspect glue, the panels flew free from each other. Except the ones that Ross and I were holding on to. It was like one of those martial arts demonstrations, where a guy with a black belt chops a piece of wood in half with his bare hands to show his expertise. Only this was a man wearing a toolbelt, with a little less expertise.

What followed was a stream of profanities at a velocity I never would have thought possible, echoed by the sound of falling wood, more tragic than the timber of a great Douglas fir in the forest. At least the Douglas fir could be repurposed as something grand, and in its place a new tree could be planted. Such was not the case with that mystery wood of the ill-designed desk. I know this because I attended its cremation later that evening at the firepit in our backyard. I believe in the eulogy, my dad referred to it as a "goddamn arsehole."

CHAPTER 13

I Should Have Learned How to Fix a Bike

In fairness to my dad, his woodworking got better and better over the years. So much so that later in life, everyone in the family could look forward to receiving a holiday gift that my dad had made and my stepmom, Barb, had painted. Tables. Chests. Yes, even DESKS (albeit desks with screws rather than nails . . . and no glue whatsoever). Our house in Toronto has Slim's creations throughout, including a rocking horse that Dad originally made for my nephew Kody (who is now in his thirties) and Scarlett still rides today. It may be the most solid thing he ever crafted (including me).

But more than building stuff with wood, Slim was really good at fixing bikes. In fact, he ran successful bike repair shops in Toronto and London that my brother Ross and I both worked at, one of us (Ross) more successfully than the other.

95

I was given ample opportunity to learn the craft of bike repair from my dad and my brother when I was ten years old and we moved to London. There, Slim opened up JR's Bike Shop, which stood for "John, Ross, Steve." Perhaps I was angry that my initial was after the apostrophe, but instead of learning how to fix bikes, I picked up a different, but no less valuable, life lesson: if you fail to learn to do something properly, out of some sort of stubborn resistance to making an effort, people don't ask you to do it anymore. And it really frees up your weekend.

Take truing, or straightening, a wheel, for instance. It's pretty straightforward, really. You take the tube out from inside the tire, place the wheel in a truing stand and tighten the spokes of the wheel using a special wrench until the rim doesn't rub against the sides of the truing stand anymore. After that, you replace the tube and the tire on the rim and put the wheel back on the bike and the job is done.

Instead, I would take out the tube, place the wheel in the truing stand, spin it around for a while like the Big Wheel on the *Price Is Right*, then replace the tube and put the tire back on the bike. Job not done at all.

This resulted in a wheel that was still not straight, or true—in other words, a lie. Which my dad would then have to fix himself. And try as he did to teach me the true way to true, I wouldn't listen. True story.

Why wouldn't I listen? I have no idea, really. I just didn't want to be stuck in a bike shop. I wanted to go out and play baseball (the one sport I played quite well as a kid). I'm not sure if this was just my issue or if all ten-year-old boys are arseholes. But I can't imagine how frustrating it must have been for my dad to try to teach me a worthwhile skill—something he was very good at—only to have me block myself from learning it so I could go do something that I enjoyed much more. My dad never made a big deal out of it, though. A few years later, he even coached my baseball team. In the end I didn't end up being a high-paid professional ballplayer and I *did* cost my dad quite a bit of money and time by not fixing bikes properly in his shop. So I should probably send him some money while I'm thinking about all this.

It makes me wonder how hard a parent should push his children in teaching them valuable life skills. And how often do kids wilfully refuse to learn how to do something in order to get out of doing it?

Off the top of my head, the other things I remember my dad trying to teach me that I never really made an effort to learn were cross-country skiing (too cold), golf (too time-consuming), plumbing (too close to the toilet), swimming (too scared of water), canoeing (refer to swimming), skating (too painful for my flat feet), sales (too hard) and the one that must have hurt him the most, long-distance running (I actually really tried at that one—too tiring).

Now that I think about it, my dad was constantly trying to teach me things when I was a kid, and I was constantly trying not to listen to what he was saying. This might have been because I was angry with my parents when they got divorced, or it could just have been that I was born set in my ways. In the case of the latter (since Nancy and I are still happily married as I write this), I can already see my stubborn streak showing up in Scarlett.

Now, the list of things I've tried to teach Scarlett so far isn't terribly extensive. This is partly because she's only five years old and mostly because I don't know how to do many things well. But one thing we do spend a *lot* of time doing together is reading and making up stories. (Actually, this is technically two things. So another thing

I don't know how to do is keep track of how many things I'm doing.)

Scarlett is an avid reader. And by that, I mean she *loves* when my wife and I read to her. But she is now getting to a stage where she should be reading more books herself and I can sense her not wanting to do it. Nancy reads with her in both French and English, so Scarlett's young brain already has twice the workload that mine ever had when I was her age. But the frustration my daughter expresses when she is trying to sound out a word—or worse yet, is *corrected* on something—is reminiscent of a baseball manager arguing with an umpire or a driver who has just been cut off. Maybe it's just me, but when drivers cut me off, it's amazing how many acceptable new ways I can find to curse at them that my dad would never have bothered trying:

CAR CUTS ME OFF.

Me: Aaaargh! Fu—

Scarlett: What's wrong, Daddy?

Me: That driver is a fu . . . ndamentally bad person. That's all, honey.

Anyway, Scarlett HATES being corrected when she's reading, even though all we're doing is trying to help her learn. I tell her that the more she can read by herself, the more things she can learn! But Scarlett doesn't want to spend her time reading, so she refuses to even try. No matter how hard I work to convince her that reading is important, it just isn't important to her right now. She wants to enjoy the story without having to think about the elements that go into it (that is, the written words). It's very much like my relationship with beer. I love a good beer, but I don't care how they make it. Granted, Scarlett is five, and I was ten years old when I was refusing to learn from my dad. But I think this is still a fair comparison because I believe Scarlett is at least twice as smart as I was at her age. Hence, she should already be accomplishing things that I didn't do until ten.

This nicely sums up my knowledge of math and genetics.

My point is that I think Scarlett is ready to be challenged when it comes to reading, but she doesn't *want* to be challenged. So there are a couple of ways I can deal with this as her dad. I can let her coast along until she's ready for more reading, hoping that she picks it up as soon as possible, or Nancy and I can challenge her to read a little bit more every day, making sure she actually knows words and isn't just memorizing stories (a skill she has demonstrated she is well able to do). This will frustrate her (I know this because it already has), but ultimately I think that picking places to challenge your children intellectually is the best gift you can give them.

My dad didn't always do this with me. He allowed me not to do things I didn't want to do when I was very young and now I regret not knowing how to do those things. If I'd listened to my dad, I'd have more valuable skills I could be teaching Scarlett.

All of this is to say that one way or another, Scarlett is going to learn how to fix a bike. As soon as I teach myself what I could have learned over thirty years ago.

CHAPTER 14

It's Like Riding a Bike

Whenever people talk about learning something that is relatively straightforward or relearning something that they technically already know, they say, "It's like riding a bike." Which I suppose means "Don't worry—you'll just magically remember how to do it." But that presumes that everyone (1) knows how to ride a bike, and (2) enjoyed the experience of learning how to ride that bike. Those are awfully big presumptions.

Case in point, my dad taught me to ride a bike when I was four years old (one of the few lessons that actually stuck), and he very much approached the task from the perspective that I already knew how to do it. This might have been because I was the youngest of five sons and all my older brothers had already been riding bikes for quite some time. Or he may have just honestly believed that all small humans were born knowing how to ride a bike. It's also possible that he was just so proud of the three-speed bike he had built for me from parts he had lying around the shop that it never occurred to him I should learn to ride on a smaller bicycle, with only one speed and two additional (training) wheels.

Whatever the case, it was with great expectations that my dad encouraged four-year-old me to hop on my three-speed bicycle, with the seat post hiked up as high as it could go, so that he could teach me how to ride and still not miss the kickoff of the football game in fifteen minutes.

The first challenge of the lesson was that I couldn't even come close to getting on the seat of the bike. It was roughly akin to a jockey trying to mount a Clydesdale. After I'd failed a few attempts at stepping over the bike (and one attempt at taking a running jump onto it), my frustrated father finally deployed the kickstand and peevishly placed me on the precarious perch. Problem solved! My butt was on the seat and my arms, when I stretched out completely, could reach the handlebars. But my feet were . . . about halfway to the pedals.

"Goddammit!" Dad said, I think to himself. But since it was out loud and I could hear it, I assumed at the time that it was intended for me.

"Sorry, Dad," I replied, apologizing for not having the ability to grow immediately to the height required for this bicycle.

"It's okay," he said. "I'll just lower the seat."

Then he headed for the garage, leaving me ever so briefly balanced on the bike. Until I wasn't. I fell off, the bike fell *on* me and my small child brain told me it was time to cry. But my large dad quashed that instinct with a quick glance over his shoulder.

"Goddammit, Stephen, you're not even MOVING yet!"

Fair point.

My cry froze in my throat and I mustered up another apology for not having a better landing technique when left on an elevated platform that was leaning to one side.

Eventually, Dad returned from the garage, wrench in hand, to readjust the seat. He then had me stand beside the bike to compare the height of my butt to the height of the seat (something that arguably should have been done in the first place, which I made a mental note of but didn't relay out loud). As it turned out, the seat had to be brought down to its lowest setting, and even then, it was still impossible for my feet to touch the ground when I was sitting on it. They could reach the pedals, though, which my dad pointed out was what they would be doing when I was riding the bike anyway. It made sense at the time. It also made sense that I would need to get *on* the bike by myself, without Dad's help. So he showed me how to lean it up against the front steps of our house to mount it. Again, this all checked out at the time. To get on your bike, you simply leaned it against something high and jumped onto the seat. No problem. Now what?

"Well," Dad said as he held on to the handlebars (I could still barely reach them by leaning forward), "now you pedal."

And so, that's what I did.

I began to pedal, precariously, since my toes could barely reach the bottom of one pedal after the other foot pushed down at the top of its revolution. As a matter of fact, I'm not sure I *could* maintain contact. So I developed an odd lopsided technique, whereby one foot would begin its downward pedalling motion while the other foot briefly lost contact with its pedal, only to be reunited a short time later. Like a cellphone that cuts out every few seconds. It doesn't make the conversation impossible, but it sure is irritating.

Dad saw nothing odd about this, however, because he was too busy yelling, "Jesus, Stephen! Keep the handlebars straight!"

The handlebars, of course, were another matter entirely. I mean, really, all you're doing is holding on to them, right? What could go wrong? Well, when you can barely *reach* them, plenty can go wrong, as it turns out. We've all seen first-time drivers behind the wheel of a car. Their hands are firmly at the 10 and 2 positions, knuckles wrapped tight like they're grasping two winning lottery tickets. Well, imagine if you couldn't reach that wheel and the vehicle you were trying to control was going over bumpy terrain and gaining speed because your dad had decided that the best place for you to learn how to ride an oversized bike was down a steep hill.

"I'm TRYING!" I remember yelling as the bike swerved and I fought desperately to keep both hands on the handlebars, since there was only one foot on the pedals at any one time.

But I have to give credit where credit is due: my dad did yell words of encouragement between the berating and the blasphemy.

"There you go, son! You're getting it now!" I remember hearing as my outstretched hands became more stable and my path more straight.

I *was* getting it! I was riding a bike! And fast, too, because the hill was getting steeper and steeper. My feet were having more trouble keeping up with the pedals (we hadn't covered the gliding option in the lesson yet), so I was chugging my chubby little legs as fast as they would go. I held on to the handlebars for dear life. Thank God my dad was holding on to the seat behind me!

"Dad! How do I slow down?" I yelled. "Dad!!! HOW DO I SLOW DOOOWWWWWWN?!"

My dad didn't answer, which I remember thinking was a bit weird.

So I turned around to ask him face to face. That's when I realized that Dad wasn't answering me because he was no longer holding on to the bike. He was nowhere near me, in fact. He had let go sometime back—at least twenty yards uphill, to be more specific. And he was looking down at me proudly . . . until he saw me turn around to look at him, at which point he yelled something that sounded like "Oook ot!"

I turned back around just in time to see that I was about to become airborne. As my bike veered right and the road dropped off into a ditch, I remember hearing my dad yell the piece of information that may have saved my life: "LET GO!"

Not many human children get to experience the miracle of self-propelled flight. Certainly not ones who woke up that morning merely hoping to learn how to ride a bike. But that day, four-year-old Steve Patterson briefly became a bird. I flew clear of the bike. Though my legs continued to pump, there were no pedals. I truly felt like a fledgling must feel the first time it flaps its wings and leaves the nest. I remember thinking, "BIKE RIDING IS SOOOO MUCH FUUUUUUUUUNNNN!"

And then I remember my dad leaning over me.

"Jesus Christ, Stephen! When you're riding your bike, you *never* look backwards! Good thing you landed in soft gravel!" (Note: No gravel is truly soft.) "Are you okay?"

I can't honestly remember how I responded. Partly because I was so young, partly because it was so long ago and mostly, I'm sure, because these were the days before mandatory bike helmets, so I was almost certainly concussed. But I'd like to think I responded the way any carefree child would: by saying, "Again! Again!"

———

Now fast-forward a good forty years.

Four-year-old Scarlett was enrolled in Pedalheads summer camp to learn how to ride a bike. Of course, I protested to Nancy that I should be the one to teach her and carry on the proud Patterson family tradition. Then I remembered my dad's lessons and I thought, "Well, a focused bike-riding camp couldn't hurt. At least not as much as being thrown clear after hurtling down a steep hill." So off to Pedalheads, Scarlett and I went.

The camp's goal was ambitious but fair: get each kid to ride his or her bike, without training wheels, within a week.

I was excited for Scarlett. Most kids her age in the neighbourhood seemed to pedal around with their training wheels for weeks or months, which is a problem because once you get used to the extra support of training wheels, it takes longer to develop the balance required for riding on two wheels. Also, the course was taught by young men and women in their late teens and early twenties who were probably more patient than I would have been. And they were definitely better suited to the back-bending agility that bike-riding instruction requires (no wonder my dad let me go at the top of that hill).

All Scarlett needed now was a bike!

We had a small used bike that some friends had given us, and Scarlett had been out on it, with training wheels attached, a few times. But biking camp was a milestone, so I decided she should mark the occasion with a new bike of her own choosing. It was also an opportunity to teach her a lesson in financial responsibility, so Scarlett bought the bike herself with funds she had accumulated from birthday presents, profits from a lemonade stand and the proceeds of returning Daddy's empty beer bottles. It's not important which source provided the most revenue. The point is that Scarlett had saved up enough to buy a new bike and a new helmet. She was proud of her purchases and more than ready to learn how to ride!

So off to Pedalheads we went. Or I guess I should say *she* went. That was the first time I realized that sometimes my little girl wasn't going to need me around. When I dropped her off at the schoolground, where a bunch of kids she didn't know were wheeling around (along with her best friend, Tegan, which certainly made things easier), not only didn't she linger around for a hug of reassurance, but she looked back at me with a puzzled expression and said, "Daddy, why are you STILL here?"

Reminder that Scarlett was four years old at this point. Not fourteen.

I skulked away from the camp thinking, "Well, at least she hasn't started dating yet," and hoping she would do okay with her teenage instructor, Emma. But when I returned in the afternoon to pick her up, she looked crestfallen.

"What's wrong, Scar Scar?" I asked.

"Emma says my bike is too big," she replied, not quite crying but not quite not crying either.

With that, I realized how much like my dad I was, even if I didn't want to admit it. I had bought Scarlett (actually *she* had bought herself) the bike she wanted at the same shop where I'd bought my own bike. It looked great and came with training wheels on, and the shop owner had assured us that this was better than getting a bike the child couldn't grow with. I had agreed with him because Scarlett looked so happy riding it. She had also bought a matching skateboarding helmet painted like a watermelon, which I was assured was more safe than a traditional bike helmet because it could withstand multiple impacts. Given my family biking history, this was mandatory.

But none of that mattered.

The bike was too big for her right now. At Pedalheads camp, the kids had to do drills where their feet were flat on the ground and Scarlett simply couldn't do them on her brand-new bike. It wasn't quite a "send your helmetless kid hurtling down a hill" kind of screw-up, but it was a "your kid is going to be embarrassed in front of other kids because of you" screw-up. I hadn't planned to cause one of those moments until she was at least ten years old.

Of course, Nancy had the perfect and immediate solution. "That's okay," she said. "We'll bring her old bike to camp, too." That way, Scarlett could do some of the drills with a bike that would allow her feet to touch the ground and then use her new bike for the drills with training wheels.

I knew this idea was genius because it would never have occurred to me.

The next morning, I drove Scarlett back to camp with both her shiny new bike with training wheels and her less shiny but smaller bike without training wheels. This way, she went from having an old baby bike to having a cool new bike, PLUS a bike she used only when she didn't want to get the new one dirty. Every kid in camp thought she was the coolest, and Scarlett did indeed learn to ride the smaller bike, without training wheels, within a week! Mission accomplished. Dad's mistake fixed by Mom's perfect solution number 4,387.

Later that summer, with Scarlett now approaching her fifth birthday and asking every day to ride the big bike without training wheels, we headed to a basketball court in our neighbourhood park. I had reluctantly agreed to let her try it, but I'd promised I would be right beside her all the way along. Plus, we were only doing it on the basketball court, where there were no cars and (more importantly to me) no giant hills or ditches. It took us a few laps around the court with me holding on to the back of the seat, but soon I was able to let go and off she went! Scarlett was riding the big bike all by herself! She even learned the art of the handbrake, a new accessory that her old bike didn't have. And not long after learning how to stop, she learned how to use the pedal brake to *skid* to a stop, which was obviously much cooler. Of course, I couldn't help thinking that the skid stop would wear down the goddamn tires sooner (there's my dad again), but it was bringing her a lot of joy, so I decided not to say anything.

All that was left to do was show her mom what "we" had done. I called Nancy, excited, and told her to come to the park to see something special. She ran over right away and we prepared for the big show. (Scarlett loves showtime more than any child I've ever seen.) She started off slowly, gained speed, got to the corner of the court just as we had practised, turned and . . . ran directly into the pole holding the basketball net and then fell off her bike.

It was heartbreaking because of how much Scarlett had wanted to show off to her mom, but it was also hilarious. She wasn't hurt, and the "PING!" sound that the bike made when her handlebars hit the pole was the perfect comic beat. But not to Scarlett. When she picked herself up, she got up angry. Somehow it was my fault she had run into that pole, even though I was nowhere near her at the time.

"Daddy! Why didn't you tell me that pole was there?"

"You knew it was there, Scarlett. But you looked backwards while you were riding. When you're riding your bike, you never look backwards!"

And there it was. I had officially channelled the one piece of wisdom my dad had imparted to me forty years earlier and had passed it on to my daughter. Only she didn't have to fly through the air to learn it. Just a quick little collision with a basketball pole. My work here was done.

With that, Scarlett got back on her bike and started to ride again, flawlessly this time. Because after all, once you know how to do something, it really is just like riding a bike.

CHAPTER 15

Norah!

I remember a rhyme from my elementary school days that was generally used to mock boys who had shown some sort of romantic interest in girls:

First comes love,
Then comes marriage,
Then comes a baby in a baby carriage.

It was probably composed originally to celebrate adult couples having a baby. But in London, Ontario, in the early 1980s it was a very effective way of dissuading a boy from pursuing a romantic relationship with a girl. This was usually initiated by said boy's best friend (let's call him Ted), who wasn't ready for his buddy to go off, get married and start a family. Which frankly was a long shot at best in fifth grade, but I guess you can't be too careful.

In any case, that rhyme has stuck with me into my adult life. As I passed through romantic relationships in my twenties and then my thirties, I would always get to a point when I would have to ask myself, "Is this the person I'm going to marry? Are we going to have a baby together? Do they still call it a carriage?"

Then the woman I was with would ask me what I was talking about. I really have to stop saying my thoughts out loud.

But once I met Nancy, I knew she was "the one." I married her and then, after so many attempts, we were blessed with Scarlett. At that point, I figured I had fulfilled my destiny. (If you're wondering, Ted had been married fifteen years and had two children of his own by this point. So I think he was ready to let me go.)

Nancy was more than willing to have a little baby brother or sister for Scarlett. I, on the other hand, wasn't so sure—but not because I didn't want to have more children with Nancy. She had proven to be an incredibly devoted and fantastic mom. It's just that Scarlett seemed perfectly content to be an only child. I say this because of how much she revelled in our undivided attention and also because she was often a living, breathing barrier to creating a sibling.

Seriously.

Intimate moments with your spouse aren't just tricky when there's a baby in the house—they're damn near impossible. Even when the baby is not physically attached to the mother, he or she is never far away. Plus, when the mother is the sole food source for the baby, it is difficult to find romantic time in between feedings. We've all heard the expression "Don't shit where you eat." Well, imagine trying to get busy where your baby eats. It's basically like your dad trying to seduce your lunch. Which is somehow more disturbing than what the adolescent kid did with his dessert in the *American Pie* movie (google it).

There's also the fatigue factor. Being a mother to a newborn is the most tiring job in the world, even though most mothers will never admit it (some do, though, and I don't blame them—if I had to go through what a newborn's mom does, I would complain to everyone at every opportunity). People talk about being on call for various jobs and how difficult that is. Surgeons may be called upon to save a patient's life at a moment's notice. Firefighters and emergency responders are called upon to confront situations that most of us would instinctively run away from. The Canadian Senate may, at some point, do something. But as the mom of a newborn, you are literally on call 24/7. You are always nurturing, teaching, comforting and protecting your baby. On the rare occasions you do have a moment to rest, you don't. Instead, you use that time to research what to do with your baby next. And when you do finally go to sleep, you're dreaming about your baby until the second she needs you again, at which point you immediately burst back into action, catering to her needs. (Unless, of course, you have a full staff of people to take care of your baby for you. But that's not really parenting. That's outsourcing.)

It's exhausting just to think about it. Which is probably why many dads don't. They try to get on with their lives the same way they did before the baby arrived. They go to work. They socialize with friends. Some of them go golfing for hours at a time. (If I had told Nancy I was going golfing within the first few months of Scarlett's birth, she would have kicked me in the crotch so hard that the idea of having another baby would have been deemed null and void anyway.)

Plus, even on the occasions when you're both awake while the baby is asleep, you're rarely in a bed that the baby is *not* in. (Scarlett slept in our bed most of the early years of her life and continues to do so whenever she can. Whoever says you shouldn't do this does not have a child as persistent as Scarlett in their house.) And when the timing seems right for a little loving, there is simply nothing that ruins the mood more than the sound of your baby crying. To a mother, it is an urgent emergency call: "MOMMY! HELP ME RIGHT NOW!" To the father, it is a damning accusation: "HEY! WHAT ARE YOU DOING TO MY MOMMY!?" Either way, it makes an erection go away faster than it took to conceive the baby in the first place.

On the off chance that the father in this scenario is able to stay focused on the amorous activity and continue, he is setting himself up for failure and will be airborne in seconds. That's because the mother, upon hearing her baby in distress, has the strength of . . . well, a mother, which is equal to that of at least ten fathers. Long story short, I remember at least one occasion when Nancy and I were in the moment when we heard Scarlett cry. Nancy instinctively threw me off so hard, I'm pretty sure my arse hit the ceiling. When she returned to bed with the baby in tow, she asked me why I was wincing in pain, while Scarlett looked at me with a mischievous grin that seemed to say, "I am watching you, old man."

Nancy, Scarlett and I lived like this for over four years. Nancy was on call for Scarlett the entire time (while somehow still managing the logistics of my comedy career) and every day I was getting more and more used to and comfortable with being Scarlett's dad (and Scarlett's dad alone). Nancy and I still talked about having another baby, but if there's one thing I know about making babies, it's that you can't just talk about it. You have to actually be able to make the time to make the baby. And that's difficult when you already have a baby taking up most of that time.

I marvel at couples who do this. One couple we know had two

sons in such rapid succession I wondered if they were actually slightly delayed twins. (One term I've heard for this is "Irish twins," although I'm not sure of the origin. Perhaps it means that Irish people are very horny, or that they're better at ignoring their existing children to make new ones. Nancy and I are both of Irish descent and this term didn't apply to us.)

Another important thing to know is that having a baby after several miscarriages doesn't mean that you won't have more miscarriages while trying to have baby number two. So it was that Nancy, in the midst of the exhausting roller coaster that comes with being a new mother, had to deal with another heartbreaking loss. The experience is different when you have an infant at home already as it comes with the new challenge of having to suspend your own grief.

Nancy had to go to the same hospital where Scarlett was born, St. Joseph's in Toronto, for the procedure while I stayed home with Scarlett, who was two years old at the time. Of course, she didn't know what was going on, but she sure knew that her mommy wasn't there when she wanted her and that Daddy was going to have to do what he could, which clearly wasn't enough.

Nancy had pumped some breast milk before heading to the hospital and I was doing my best to approximate the breastfeeding experience with a baby bottle, but let's be honest, looking up at my face for comfort when you're used to looking up at Nancy's has to be . . . well, discomforting.

So while Nancy was at the hospital dealing with the devastating physical and emotional toll of another miscarriage, I was trying to be "mommy" to Scarlett—and failing miserably. At some point late in the night, Nancy called us to check in. I wanted to tell her that I was sorry I couldn't be there with her, that Scarlett was doing fine and that, for once, she should just focus on herself. But what came out, against the sound of Scarlett's screams in the background, was that our baby needed her mommy. RIGHT NOW!

So Nancy did something that says everything about her as a mother. It's something that I'm sure many moms would do for their babies and that no one would ever believe until they witnessed it for themselves. She sang Scarlett's favourite song, "Puff, the Magic Dragon," into the phone several times and lulled our baby to sleep. From a hospital room where she was being treated because a pregnancy that she desperately wanted would not result in the baby that she desperately wanted, Nancy lulled her inconsolable child to sleep. Hell, to be honest, she did it so well, I almost nodded off myself. Then she went back to the awful experience she was having to live through yet again.

After that miscarriage, I'm not sure we talked again about having another baby. I knew Nancy still wanted to and I knew I loved being a dad and I think I was getting pretty good at it. (I had also learned a pretty decent version of "Puff, the Magic Dragon" by that point.) Even Scarlett was starting to talk about how neat it would be to have a little sister. (She would also "tolerate" a little brother. But a little sister would be "much better." Her actual words.) But I was worried that another miscarriage might be too much for Nancy. Or maybe it would just be too much for me. Obviously, she is tougher than I am.

So we continued our lives in love and marriage, with a baby, in a baby carriage (actually it was a Bugaboo luxury baby stroller that we had paid too much for). Scarlett continued to grow and flourish, Nancy continued to be a world-class mom and I continued to try to become a better dad with varying degrees of success. Nancy had also begrudgingly begun to pack up clothes and other things that Scarlett had grown out of to donate to charitable organizations or give to friends who were expecting babies.

But it turned out, the universe had other plans.

Right around Christmas 2018, Nancy told me she was pregnant again!

A lot went through my mind. The first thought was, "Really? I don't even remember us doing it." Which, of course, I said out loud.

"Well we *did*, and I *am!*" Nancy said, smiling through slightly gritted teeth.

My other thoughts, which I did manage to keep inside, were:

1. "THANK GOD THIS IS HAPPENING!" Because I had indeed been praying for it. And that was closely followed by:
2. "GOD, IS THIS HAPPENING?" Because I had accepted the fact that Scarlett was going to be our only child, and I was perfectly okay with that. And finally:
3. "GOD, PLEASE LET THIS HAPPEN!" Because emotionally I don't think I could have gone through another miscarriage. Even if Nancy could.

The next months were as giddy, nerve-racking, cautious and finally joyous as any I've ever experienced. Nancy's pregnancy progressed perfectly, and soon we had gone beyond the point we had passed only once before (not a great slogan if you're a *Star Trek* fan, I know, but fitting when it comes to pregnancy). By the summer, Nancy was fully pregnant and ready for baby number two and Scarlett was more than ready to be a big sister. Now, finally, I was cautiously optimistic.

As we entered July 2019, we were ready to become parents again. Well, a little more prepared than we were the first time anyway. For one thing, we had our close friends Bruce and Lindsay ready to take care of Scarlett when the moment came. We also knew we weren't going to have Nancy go past her due date as she had with Scarlett. Given our history, our family doctor didn't think that would be a good idea. So Nancy would be induced if the baby didn't arrive on time. We also didn't want Nancy going through labour for twenty-seven hours again. I think anyone who has been through that experience will tell you that once is more than enough.

Almost exactly five years after Scarlett's birth, we headed back to St. Joseph's Hospital feeling considerably more confident than we had back then. For one thing, we hadn't just done hypothetical training on being parents—we had been raising a real live baby for five years! Also, we had done all the necessary paperwork to arrange a room beforehand instead of scrambling when we arrived at the hospital, and that meant Nancy wouldn't have to spend some of her time in labour in the hallway (strongly *not* recommended). And most importantly, this time I had packed TWO large portions of spaghetti and hidden one from Nancy.

I have to say that the second birth went a lot more smoothly than the first. For one thing, our nurse, Kelsey, was able to remain with us throughout the labour and delivery (just one of the advantages of having a labour that doesn't go longer than a staff shift). Also, our family doctor was at the hospital to perform the delivery (just one of the advantages of having a family doctor who is also an ob-gyn). And finally, the labour was several hours shorter!

As a matter of fact, instead of the false starts and the "push, push, push, then pause" that Nancy had gone through with Scarlett, this time we actually had to hold her back from pushing because our doctor wasn't in the delivery room yet. Nurse Kelsey actually had to say, "Hold on!" and then go looking for our doctor, leaving me and Nancy staring awkwardly at each other. She was grasping my hand with a grip that would have crushed a bowling ball, but I decided not to express my discomfort given her current position. I was more worried that if she did push at that point, the baby would suddenly shoot out like Gonzo from the cannon on *The Muppet Show*, and I would have to make a diving catch. The thought actually made me smile through the pain of my hand being crushed and Nancy, in an amazing moment of reading my thoughts, actually said, "I hope the doctor gets here before I shoot the baby across the room!"

Once you've been together for a while, you start to share the same brain.

Moments later, Nurse Kelsey was back, along with our doctor, Shawna Hills, and another doctor who was along to assist her. It made for an awkward moment as the training doctor was introduced to Nancy.

Dr. Hills: "Nancy, this is Dr. So-and-So." (The actual doctor has an actual name, but it escapes me right now. Sorry, Doctor! I was kind of preoccupied with a baby being born and everything.) "She is a resident here and will be assisting me."

Nancy: "Hello, Doctor. This is my vagina, and a baby's about to come out of it."

The last moments of the birth were indeed what you see portrayed in the movies. Our doctor said, "Push." Nancy pushed, and our baby came out.

Norah Kathleen Patterson was born on July 31, 2019, weighing in at seven pounds, twelve ounces. If she'd been one day later, she would have shared the same birth month as Scarlett. Somehow she knew this wasn't something her big sister would approve of.

I remember cutting the cord like an old pro. I remember not being scared to hold my baby girl, because now I had almost five years of practice with her big sister. I remember the joy I felt was just as great as when Scarlett was born, because once again, I wasn't sure this day would ever come. I remember stroking Nancy's head and telling her how proud I was of her. Again.

The doctors, meanwhile, were commenting on how round Norah's head was in a very complimentary way. "Wow! That's a great round head!" Apparently, a lot of us come into the world with non-round-shaped heads. I'm pretty sure mine was a rhombus.

Then I remember our doctor saying, directly to me, "Another little girl! Maybe you can go for three!"

Which made me think to myself, "God, no! I'd take a vasectomy right now if someone in this hospital would do it."

That's when Nancy, Nurse Kelsey and both doctors all turned to look at me, stone-faced.

Goddammit, I had said that out loud.

CHAPTER 16

Two Are Better Than One?

As soon as people found out we were expecting a second child, the overwhelming response was "Congratulations! Two are better than one!" But thinking back, everyone who said that had either one or zero children.

At first, Scarlett was over the moon about having a little sister. After Norah's birth, I went and picked her up from Bruce and Lindsay's house and brought her to the hospital. We'd already told Scarlett that we were naming her sister Norah, so she came into the hospital screaming, "Norah!!! Where's my sister, Norah?!" Which might have been a nuisance to others, but let's be honest, in the birthing wing of a hospital, there are a lot more urgent screams to tend to.

When we got to the room, Scarlett ran to her baby sister—after I'd made sure she washed her hands, of course (pro dad tip number 1 of older child handling baby child). Immediately, she wanted to hold her. Nancy explained the importance of properly supporting the head (after all, it was apparently gloriously round), and Scarlett sat proudly beside her mom and gazed down into her baby sister's face with a look of love I'd seen her show only to her favourite dolls and me whenever she wanted dessert. Norah opened her eyes, looked up at Scarlett, who is more and more like a miniature Nancy every day, and probably thought, "Wow, Mom! You look a lot younger today!"

When we brought Norah home from the hospital, it was a little different than when we'd returned home with Scarlett. At that time, our friends Craig and Erica had decorated the house with "Welcome Home, Scarlett" banners—which Scarlett couldn't read and Nancy admired for a full three seconds before heading to the nursery we had

Norah arrives and Scarlett becomes a big sister.

set up so that she and the baby could continue their bonding. But Norah didn't get decorations. Or her own room. Her crib (which had also been Scarlett's) was stationed on the far side of our bedroom, which is on the top floor of our Toronto townhouse. To be honest, it's a big enough room that the crib doesn't get in the way, and babies don't really need their own rooms anyway. As long as they have a dark, quiet area to sleep, it's rare for them to complain about a lack of square footage or a door of their own.

But it is interesting how shortchanged the second child can be. For Scarlett, we bought all new stuff, including a crib, a stroller and a car seat. There were kickass baby showers in Toronto and Montreal (where Nancy's parents live). And we converted our spare room into Scarlett's room.

Norah came home from the hospital in Scarlett's old car seat, lay down in Scarlett's old crib (which we had also loaned out to friends, whose two sons had used it in between) and settled in for a nap in our bedroom. And there were no baby showers because everyone had bought us stuff the first time around. Now that I think about it, I should have at least thrown a keg party with a "box of diapers" cover charge.

There weren't even a lot of new outfits for Norah, since we still had all the ones we'd bought for Scarlett. This is a pattern that will be repeated over the course of the next seventeen years or so, I'm sure. Having grown up the youngest of five sons, I know a thing or two about hand-me-down clothes—though not necessarily baby clothes. I'm pretty sure my brothers *ate* all theirs. Once I entered first grade, however, I wore clothes that my much older brothers had once worn, causing my confused classmates to ask questions like

"What's *The Howdy Doody Show*?" (It's a children's show that had been popular up until eleven years before I was born. Somehow I still had the T-shirt.) Or, "Why is that bunny wearing a tie?" (The *Playboy* logo was on an old smoking jacket that I wore as a super-hero cape.)

When your newborn daughter wears your now five-year-old daughter's old baby clothes, it feels very much like you've gone back in time. Plus, Norah looks pretty much exactly like Scarlett did as a baby. So there are moments when I see her in an outfit, think she is Scarlett and wonder if I just dreamt that we'd had another baby.

But those moments fade quickly when Norah, Scarlett and sometimes Nancy break into tears simultaneously.

As a matter of fact, Scarlett had her first breakdown not long after Norah came home from the hospital. It was the next day, actually, and she complained that she just didn't feel as though she was "getting undivided attention anymore." Scarlett sometimes says things that make me think she read all the parenting books that I didn't. She also pointed out that Norah's crying at night was "irritating." I bit my lip so that I didn't respond, "It was just as irritating when you did it."

Nancy, of course, tries to oblige Scarlett at every opportunity. Yet her attention is rarely, if ever, undivided, since Norah is always near her and/or actually attached to her. This means that my job as supportive husband and dad is to give Scarlett the attention that Nancy is unable to provide. The problem is, Scarlett doesn't want *my* attention. She wants Nancy's. Which, of course, I take as a personal insult. Nancy has to point out to me that I shouldn't take things so personally, and that I am not, in fact, a five-year-old child or a baby.

So what is the solution? How can you, as a parent, give two different children your undivided attention? Well, in a two-parent, two-child household, the answer is to transition to man-to-man defence from zone coverage. With zone coverage, both parents stay in the approximate vicinity of one child, blocking all dangers and escape routes. Man-to-man (or adult-to-child) defence, where each parent is assigned a particular child to look after, is the ideal coverage.

Those parents who say that two are better than one are probably strong man-to-man defenders. That is, there are usually two of them on hand, and in most cases, they can move faster than an infant or toddler to create a formidable barricade against any sort of dangerous situation. But for most households, it's not possible to have two parents present at all times. Most often, there will just be one tired parent present. And if that one parent is the husband, and he's with a baby who's used to breastfeeding and a five-year-old who needs almost constant playtime, there is a high probability of all hell breaking loose. In those situations, all game plans go out the window and you have to improvise.

On the other hand, when the two children are left with just their mother—or specifically, my daughters with *their* mother—everything seems to function at pretty much maximum efficiency.

For me, the more I can equate parenting to sports, the better the chance I have of succeeding at it. For example, the expression "It's not over until it's over" refers to trying to come back when your team is behind in a game. But in parenting, it also means encouraging your kids to finish things, like eating a meal, brushing their teeth or saying goodbye to grandparents on a video call before running out of the room. "When the going gets tough, the tough get going" can mean either rising to a challenge or "JUST PUT ON YOUR GODDAMN SHOES SO WE CAN LEAVE THIS GODDAMN HOUSE!" (That's me channelling my dad.) And perhaps my favourite, "Three strikes and you're out!" refers to the end of a failed at-bat in baseball, but it's also the maximum number of times you should have to repeat yourself to a five-year-old. Sure, there are parents out there who say, "I don't want to have to repeat myself at all," but those parents are not being realistic. Parenting is all about repeating yourself. It can be incredibly frustrating, whether your kids really don't hear you the first time, hear you but don't understand what you're saying, or hear and understand you perfectly well, but choose to ignore you. Once you've told a child the same thing three times in a row, though, then they're out. (Not out of the house, of course. That's a bit harsh—unless they're in their twenties, in which case, it's fair game.) But with actual children-aged children, the three-strikes rule may, for example, be applied to toys, especially stuffed animals. If we have to tell Scarlett three times to put away a particular toy, then that toy is going in the garbage. Of course, you don't actually throw the toy in the garbage—you just hide it until your point is proven. I learned this lesson right after I threw away an expensive toy.

I should also note here that Nancy claims she has to tell me to do some things four times before I react. I have no idea how many times she has told me this.

Since Norah's arrival, my re-entry into the household after a few days away has become much more difficult. If I'm out of town to perform, it used to be that Nancy would put Scarlett to bed at a set time, Scarlett would fall asleep, and Nancy could either sleep with her or enjoy a little bit of quiet time. During these rare moments, she would often watch *Survivor*—a show whose premise and title I really don't understand. Why? Because none of the participants have their children with them, that's why. Any adult can connive his way through other conniving adults or occasionally work with them to achieve his own selfish goals. But put a family with two small kids on a deserted island for a month and see if THEY survive. Now that's a show! (By the way, if you're a TV producer who ends up making this show, I am in no way volunteering MY family. But if the show becomes a success, I would like some royalties, please. Thank you.)

Anyway, things are much more difficult now when I come back home after a long trip because Nancy and the girls have established their own routine. This generally means Nancy is trying to keep up with the onslaught of work emails, laundry, housecleaning and meal preparation, while somehow simultaneously teaching Norah to navigate the world and Scarlett to keep up with her schoolwork. Her only fighting chance is to start the bedtime ritual early and hope that Norah falls asleep quickly and Scarlett follows her soon after. It is *not* an easy thing to accomplish on your own. But I've learned that a dad who is not used to the program and comes home after a few days away actually makes things more difficult.

For one thing, there's no better welcome home than the one you receive from your loving children and appreciative spouse, who are all genuinely happy to see you. The little girl is happy because she knows you probably brought her something from your trip. The baby girl is happy because you are, by default, one of her three favourite people in the world. And the spouse is happy because she sees you as reinforcements and a chance for a possible respite from solo parenting.

The problem is that when I'm back on the scene, the girls like hanging around with fun daytime daddy. Not bedtime daddy. Or bedtime mommy. In the minds of young children, sleep is fake news. No matter how much you tell them they need it, they don't believe you. So the best you can do is to let them exhaust themselves and then, once they're asleep, whisper in their ears, "See? You were wrong!"

Plus, mommies who have been home with two small children while daddy has been away will have approximately seven hundred dad-related questions for you the second you get back—many of them pertaining to things you have never heard of before: summer camp programs (when it's the middle of winter); the state of groceries in the kitchen ("We're out of milk, bread and vegetables. Can you go get some now?); and the latest neighbourhood crime report ("It says on the Junction Facebook page that strollers are getting stolen from sheds! Can you bring ours inside after you get the groceries? Also, the girls need a bath!").

This is all before I have taken off my coat.

So with all due respect to those who say two are better than one, in my experience so far, that is the dumbest thing I've ever heard.

CHAPTER 17

Hush, Little Husband, Don't Say a Word

I've already mentioned that some of the best times you'll have as a dad will be the ones when your very young children are asleep. So it only stands to reason that if you can be the parent who gets those children to sleep, you are the best spouse in the world.

When you have one baby, you can focus all your attention on getting that baby to sleep. And honestly, sleep is the only thing babies really know how to do instinctively, other than feed from a boobie, so it's pretty straightforward. But the expression "slept like a baby" is a bit of a misnomer, because babies don't sleep through the night. They get up to breastfeed every couple of hours, which means that the mom whose boobs the baby feeds from has to get up too. Therefore, if you have a friend who stays over at your house and says he slept like a baby, he and your wife have some serious explaining to do.

For a dad, there is no better way to show support to his spouse than helping to get the baby to sleep. I honestly believe that given the choice between a man with a chiselled jaw and rock-hard abs or one with an ample dad bod who can get a baby to sleep, most moms would choose the dad-bod dad nine times out of ten. But if that tenth chiselled dad with the abs ALSO has the magic touch with the baby . . . well, frankly, screw him. (And I'm sure his wife does. Regularly.)

In our house, Nancy and I do what a lot of parents do when trying to get their kids to sleep: we read to them, we play relaxing music, we sing softly. And when all that fails to work, we plead, beg and bribe. I think Scarlett was two years old the first time I openly offered her money if she would just go to sleep. My plea went something like this: "Scarlett, if you just go to sleep right now, I will give you a thousand dollars." It's how I imagine game show hosts get their children to sleep. But Scarlett just laughed at me, thinking I was kidding. Today, with a better sense of the value of money and a laser-focused campaign on getting a family dog, my savvy kid starts the bidding herself: "Hey, Daaaaddy? It's almost bedtime! For five hundred bucks, I think I can be sleepy in twenty minutes."

The poor kid doesn't realize that all the money I bribe her with is coming from her college fund anyway.

In lieu of bribery, you're going to want to have one or more go-to bedtime songs that you're prepared to perform approximately ten thousand times each evening. If done correctly, your kids will remember this well into adulthood. Heck, they might even use those same songs to try to get their own kids to sleep someday.

It was my mother, Kathleen, who instilled in me my first musical memories. Mom always had a great singing voice and she didn't mess around with kids' songs or nursery rhymes. She went straight for the classics, like "High Hopes" by James Van Heusen and Sammy Cahn, which is about an ant trying to move a rubber tree plant. The gist of the song is that everyone but the ant knows it's impossible for him to move a rubber tree plant, but he just keeps trying—and what do you know, he eventually succeeds!

The song was made popular by Frank Sinatra when he recorded it in 1959 for a film called *A Hole in the Head*, but as a toddler, I was led to believe that my mom had written it just for me (this is perfectly acceptable artistic licence for a parent to take). The way she sang it made me feel like I could do anything, or at least that if I were ever faced with a formidable opponent made entirely of rubber, I could beat it! Maybe not the most peaceful image to nod off to, but it did the trick.

The other song I remember my mom singing to me as a baby was "Daddy's Little Girl," which was a hit for Al Martino, another crooner who was sort of like Frank Sinatra but didn't have quite as much Italian influence in his corner. Sure, it was weird that my mom sang a song about being a little girl to a baby boy. But I think it was the song that her dad had sung to her. Or maybe it was just a reminder that after four boys, she had really wanted a girl. In any case, I remember her singing that song to me a lot. And it made much more sense when I started singing it to Scarlett and then to Norah.

As I mentioned earlier, my first go-to sleep song was the wholly inappropriate "We've Got Tonight" by Bob Seger. In my opinion, it has the perfect cadence and rhythm for inducing sleep. But I can't escape the fact that the song is about a man trying to get a woman to spend the night with him. So it's really not a great choice for a dad to sing to his baby daughter. Full disclosure: I still sometimes hum that song when I'm trying to get Norah settled down. (By humming it, I avoid the awkward lyrical implications, as well as any impending lawsuits for royalties.) I've learned that Norah has more severe FOMO (fear of missing out) than Scarlett ever did (the kid hasn't really experienced anything yet, and she still somehow misses what she is "missing out" on), and she is proving tougher to get to sleep than her sister as well. So for Norah, my song of choice is the Mexican Hat Dance, which once again is an odd choice for a lullaby, but it has a good rhythm that helps to take her to a fiesta in her mind.

Not unlike her dad, Norah is a big fan of craft beer.

Now that we have two little girls to send off to dreamland every night, our bedtime ritual is an art that Nancy and I are still trying to master. And by "master," I mean just barely survive. To make matters more challenging, both girls have very different ideas of when sleep should happen. Scarlett knows that 8 p.m. is lights out, but because Norah doesn't understand time yet, she feels there is no "bedtime."

Scarlett also loves story time right before bed, while Norah believes that story time is party time. So when Norah hears someone reading, that in her mind is an invitation to also make noise. While she doesn't understand the stories that are being told to her, she does try to fully ingest books. Literally. Norah's favourite food group right now is books. She will chew the corners of any book and attempt to rip out all the pages, which of course is an affront to authors (and I imagine books as well).

Meanwhile, with all the wisdom she has accumulated in her five years of life, Scarlett has picked up the many tricks children use to avoid going to sleep, including

- asking for a glass of water;
- chugging the glass of water she already has and asking for ANOTHER;
- having to go pee despite saying no when we asked her thirty-seven times before (mostly because she chugged her water);
- asking a couple of "quick" questions, like "Why are some people mean?" or "What is our family tree on both sides going back seven generations?";
- pleading for one more story;
- explaining that she is not even tired; and
- falling asleep two sentences into the "one more story."

Nancy and I also have very different philosophies on how to get babies to go to sleep. Nancy likes to read as many stories as possible, in both English and French, and she then lists the highlights of the day for Scarlett's dream material, much as sports channels list the highlights of the night. I, on the other hand, prefer to read two English stories, start a French story and fall asleep immediately (just as I did in French class at school). Scarlett then either falls asleep as well or calls out for her mommy, often waking me up in the process. Which is kind of rude.

But there was that *one* time I was a hero.

It was a warm fall night in Toronto. Nancy had fallen asleep with Scarlett, entrusting me to get Norah down. (Translation: She had fallen asleep from pure exhaustion and needed me to . . . well, dad up!) So I did what I almost always do when holding baby Norah: I walked around the house, swaying while cuddling her tightly against my chest. This is a risk, of course, because when babies are held against chests, they typically think it's feeding time. And as we've already covered, there's nothing more disappointing for human babies than seeking out their mother's nipple and finding their father's.

But on the bright side, the chest hair that most adult males have (unless they're competitive swimmers, perfume models or Scandinavian) holds its own comforting allure for newborns. It's like a face nest. And once tiny babies nestle into the face nest, with the soft pillows of middle-aged man boobs underneath (sure, some dads have strong pecs, but who wants to sleep on a rock-hard surface?), there's not much left for them to do other than fall asleep. Perhaps babies like the comfort and security of being cuddled by their dads, or possibly they're just going to a happier place in their newborn dreams than a hairy chest. Either way, it works! That night, I put

Norah to sleep when Nancy couldn't. It's my bases-loaded, World Series–winning home run as a dad! Never mind that Nancy has, unassisted, put both Scarlett and Norah to bed simultaneously countless times. I put one of the kids to bed that one time when Nancy was already asleep. That's the victory I hold on to.

Of course, it's not exactly heroic to serve as a soft mattress for a baby. But to the exhausted mother of that baby, you are, for a brief and shining moment, if not Superman, at least a super man.

My close friend, fellow comedian and fellow dad Dave Hemstad once held a sleeping Norah for over an hour while he watched sports. When Scarlett and his daughter Vivian ran into the room, he shushed them so they wouldn't wake the baby. For this, Nancy thanked him profusely. It was the happiest I've ever seen him. He offered to come over every Sunday during the PGA season to perform those same heroics.

This kind of guest appearance is something that fathers and especially grandfathers seem to have mastered. I call it the swoop-in-when-baby-is-already-exhausted, or SIWBIAE, syndrome. It's like helping someone on a cross-country move by picking up the last remaining lightly packed box, putting it in the back of their car and then saying, "Phew! Okay, where's that beer?"

I'm not saying that all dads and granddads are like this. I'm sure there are some out there who can put their babies and grandbabies to bed on a nightly basis without gloating about it. I salute those men. I've just never met any of them.

To all the rest of you dads, I encourage you to keep trying to get the little ones to sleep at night so you can give the moms of those little ones a much-needed break. It won't be easy. It's often a battle, and you won't always win. Sometimes you will have to give your baby back to her mother for the final push towards dreamland. But believe me, your spouse will appreciate the assist much more than she will your gloating over that one time you got the baby to sleep when she wasn't able to.

CHAPTER 18

The Kids Are Alright?

Let's rewind to my time as a baby, with a dad slightly younger than I am now and a mom who had already nurtured four other boys, including Ross, who is as many years older than me as Scarlett is older than Norah. I can't be sure, but I don't think the nurturing went quite the same for me. For one, my dad can't recall ever putting baby me to bed, but if he did, I'm sure he felt as proud as I did that time I got Norah to sleep. Also, the dynamic between little boy Ross and baby me was quite different than that between my two girls.

For instance, Scarlett often sings to Norah—songs she makes up herself, as a pledge of her undying sisterly love: "Norah, you're my baby sister/you're the best baby sister in the world/I love you soooooo much, Norah/Norah is the best!" What it lacks in rhyme, it makes up for in sentiment.

When I asked Ross if he remembered singing to me as a baby, he responded, "I don't remember you being a baby." It's this kind of blunt honesty that keeps him from a career writing Hallmark cards. However I do remember Ross singing to me while holding a flashlight under his face in our dark basement, though. It was a song by Alice Cooper called "Steven." Which is about the death of someone named Steven. Who is killed by the person who's singing the song. Ross later pointed out (after I told my dad what he had done) that the song couldn't have been about me because my name is spelled S-t-e-p-h-e-n, which, to be fair, was a pretty strong defence for a thirteen-year-old. But you can see how a young boy (I was seven years old at the time), hearing that sung to him by his older, larger brother in a dark basement with a flashlight under his face, might miss that slight detail as he peed himself in terror.

Anyway, back to my little girls. The sisterly dynamic I see developing between Scarlett and Norah is heartwarming. Norah has a big sister who is always singing her songs and doing things that look a lot more fun than . . . well, whatever those giant people (aka Mommy and Daddy) are doing. Meanwhile, Scarlett has a living, breathing doll that will likely do whatever she tells her to do in the coming years. I know this because the other day, I caught Scarlett pushing Norah in our backyard hammock at a pace that was rapidly approaching catapult intensity. Norah was screaming inside the hammock, clearly in distress, but when I told Scarlett to stop, her honest response was "Why? She likes it!"

"She doesn't like it. She's screaming," I pointed out.

"Yeah but it's a *good* scream, Daddy. You don't speak baby as well as I do. I was *just* a baby. You haven't been a baby for a long time!"

It's tough to argue with sound logic like that. I just picked Norah up out of the hammock and let Scarlett continue her game with one of her dolls. A doll that she promptly catapulted over our fence and into the neighbour's yard. So I'd met half my daily quota of "save your child's life," which every parent of an infant must fulfill. (Later that day, I fulfilled the other half by stopping Norah from diving head first out of my arms and onto the sidewalk.)

Right now, the biggest battles between the girls are for Mommy's attention (yeah, get in line, kids!). As a baby, Norah has the distinct advantage of actually needing her mom for everything. But Scarlett puts in a convincing effort to receive that coveted attention by asking Nancy (and me) for help with everything, including things I know damn well she knows how to do herself. Whether it's washing her hands or using her fork or brushing her teeth—all things I have personally taught Scarlett to do—she suddenly needs help, usually at the exact time Norah is breastfeeding.

So Nancy and I decided that Scarlett might become more independent and less needy if we gave her a little authority over Norah. For example, Nancy might say, "I'm going downstairs to get something. Can you watch Norah for a couple of minutes?" Then Scarlett is a big sister in charge.

This works . . . in two-minute bursts. Scarlett can watch her sister for that amount of time, and perhaps even include her in some playtime. Beyond that . . . well, that's how you end up with a baby in a hammock on the precipice of becoming a projectile.

To be completely honest, I don't know how the idea of babysitting is going to go over down the road. It's possible that Scarlett may become the perfect sitter, teaching Norah valuable life lessons. Or perhaps, first chance she gets, Scarlett will launch her sister into the sky.

Still, it couldn't be any worse than the one time I remember Ross babysitting me.

Ross was a fighter growing up. He was nicknamed Ox because he was basically a fully grown man by the age of eleven. As a result, many older bullies would challenge Ross to fights, thinking he was their age. He always accepted those challenges, more often than not pummelling his older opponents until he ran out of willing neighbourhood challengers (these were the days before the internet, when bullies could expand their networks to much larger areas). Ross then took up boxing for a while, and he did quite well before realizing he didn't want to be a boxer, mostly because he was also good at other things, like cooking. In particular, I remember Ox making homemade potato chips out of—wait for it—potatoes at age ten. I thought he was a wizard. As the years went by, he moved on to more complicated meals, and now he runs a very successful pasta restaurant in Nova Scotia called the Noodle Guy. (If you're ever near Port Williams in the Annapolis Valley, I highly recommend it. Tell Ross I sent you. He will smile and charge you full price.)

When I was a kid, though, Ross tried to impart his fighting knowledge, even though I was five years, eight months, several inches in height and several pounds in weight his junior. Of course, there is no way to really, truly impart fighting knowledge without the actual fighting. So what I'm saying is, Ross and I fought a lot growing up. Not all were out-and-out brawls, mind you (those would come when we were in our twenties), and eventually my older brothers stopped trying to break up our play-fights because they realized they were actually teaching moments.

I will never forget one such teaching moment that started out fun and ended up anything but. I was seven years old; Ross was thirteen and, remember, the size of a fully grown man. Our parents were out of the house, so Ross was looking after me and had decided it would be fun to record a fight where we did our own play-by-play. To enhance the authentic audio atmosphere and approximate the sound of actual boxing gloves, we hit each other with couch pillows rather than what we usually used, which were newspapers rolled up inside of socks. Now, if you're wondering why we didn't use real boxing gloves, it probably had something to do with our frugal father believing they were "too goddamned expensive." And besides, he likely never used boxing gloves when he boxed. I should stop here and note that this is terrible parental logic. Just because you didn't have proper equipment to do something when you were growing up that doesn't mean your child shouldn't have access if you can afford it. Of course you don't need expensive state-of-the-art equipment for every activity you do. But if one of your sons shows a proclivity for boxing and your other (younger, much smaller) son shows a need for protection from his brother's proclivity . . . well, all I'm saying is "GET YOUR KIDS SOME PROPER BOXING EQUIPMENT!"

Anyway, back to the teaching moment.

Ross handed me my boxing pillow, then pressed the play and record buttons on our cassette recorder (if you're too young to know what this is, google it). The tape started to roll and we began our play-fight. Ross took on the ringside-announcer persona of Stu Nahan (a famous boxing commentator made even more famous by his appearances in the *Rocky* movies), while I got ready to do my best sports-announcer-guy voice, based on the legendary Howard Cosell.

> Ross (aka Stu Nahan): Here we are for the maaaaain event. It's Rocky Marciano versus little Stevie Patterson. [I'm not sure why his persona was a famous real boxer and I was just me, but I'm over it now, I guess.] Me (aka Howard Cosell): That's right, Stu. We're here at . . . Patterson Square Garden, and the fans are excited to see these two gladiators do battle.

Both: [wild cheering sounds . . . and laughter]

At that point, we both walked to the middle of the boxing ring (living room), touched gloves (pillows) and began to fight (fight). Ross always let me throw the first few punches, confident he could avoid them. Plus, he had a much longer reach, so if he wanted to, he could just hold my forehead with his freakishly long arm and I would swing at the air between us like a cartoon character in the most demeaning of fighting moves. I remember going for the first few pillow jabs, and we were both delighted at how much it sounded like real boxing gloves.

Ross (laughing): Some short jabs there from little Stevie Patterson. Marciano blocks them, but Stevie is looking good!
Me (laughing, forgetting I'm supposed to be Howard Cosell): It's so cool! It sounds just like real boxing!
Ross (serious again): Come on now, Patterson. Get serious! We're in a fight here!
Me (as Howard Cosell again): Yes, yes, this is a true chess match as they measure each other up and dance gingerly around the ring.

Ross then threw his first jab. Not as hard as he could. Not as fast as he could. And remember, with a PILLOW. But hard enough and fast enough that it caught me square in the nose. He started to laugh as he went back into announcer mode.

Ross (laughing): Woah! Marciano landed a left jab there in the face of—

But I wasn't laughing. I was feeling the sting of getting punched in the nose—which, as anyone who has ever been punched in the nose, well, knows, is a very centring feeling. It brings you squarely into the moment. And if you have been taught to fight by your older brother, it is your cue to react by punching the source of that punch as hard as you can. It didn't matter that in this case, my opponent and teacher were one and the same.

So as Ross was still jokingly finishing his play-by-play, I wound up and, with one of my punch pillows, swung as hard as I could, hitting my brother squarely in the face, with the corner of the pillow catching his eye.

Ross stopped laughing. He didn't say anything because the punch to the eye had transformed him into the raging animal that he could become when he was punched in the eye. I realized immediately what I had done and tried to apologize.

Ross: GRRRRR!
Me: I'm sorry! I didn't mean to!

But I also had to protect myself in the way he had taught me to if I was ever in a street fight against someone much larger who didn't go down when I hit him as hard as I could.

So I kicked Ross in the nuts.

I'm not proud of it. I would never do that to my brother again. And as dishonourable fighting moves go, it is the very worst. But at that moment, it was necessary.

Ross dropped his pillows and collapsed to the ground clutching his . . . well, other pillows. I knew I had a very short window of time to escape, and I took it. I ran to the only room in the house that had a lock on the door: the bathroom. Ross groaned, not unlike a bear that had just been awoken from hibernation with a kick to the nuts. Then he came running.

> Ross: You little shit! You NEVER do that! What the hell is [groan] wrong with [groan] you!?

He grabbed the bathroom door and tried to break it down.

> Me: I'm sorry! I didn't mean to! I was just doing what you told me to do if I hit someone and they didn't fall down.
> Ross: Well, not *me*. You don't kick *me* in the nuts, you little shit!

After what seemed like several hours but was probably only two minutes of Ross trying to rip the locked door from its hinges and me holding on to it for dear life on the other side, he stopped trying to get in and went away to another part of the house. I stayed in the locked bathroom until my parents got home.

I honestly can't remember if we ever talked about the incident after that. If Ross didn't bring it up, I sure as hell wasn't going to. But I do know that I gave an exemplary review of my brother's babysitting skills to my dad, even though I was cowering in a locked bathroom when they got home.

Now, has my life experience as a dad and a brother taught me that sisters will always be gentle and take care of each other, while brothers will spend whatever time they can trying to knock each other's heads off?

Yes. Yes, it has.

CHAPTER 19

It's All Fun and Games Until . . .

The expression "It's all fun and games until someone loses an eye" was a popular mantra of my childhood. Mostly because, with a rowdy household of boys, there was a good chance one of us would be sporting an eye patch at some point.

In fairness, by the time it got down to me, there was nothing my parents hadn't seen their sons do that could potentially injure themselves or others. From swinging in trees to racing on bicycles (remember, we'd all been taught to ride by my dad) to drag racing in cars with wheels that should have been more firmly attached (I once saw the back wheel of my brother Mark's Camaro roll past him as he skidded to a stop in the ditch across the street from our house), growing up for me was very much a matter of "give it a shot and see if you live." It got to the point that if I'd told my dad I was going skydiving without a parachute, he would have barely glanced up from his newspaper to say, "Okay. Have fun, Ross." (My dad often confused our names when we were growing up, so for a while I thought my full name was John-Larry-Mark-Ross-Stephen.)

Back in the early days of the Patterson household, when it was just John and Larry, they took "fun" to a whole new level. Literally. As the story goes, my parents took my brothers to a travelling circus show when they were seven and five years old. This was back in the late 1950s, so the circus wasn't the flashy lights and brightly costumed elite athletes that we associate with Cirque du Soleil these days. There was one bright light (possibly stolen from a nearby airport) and a few brave trapeze artists performing death-defying feats high up in the air, but the main act was the animals.

Back then, most kids went to the circus to see the elephants, lions and whatever other animals the troupe could fit into a travelling caravan (not a Dodge Caravan, although I understand they do provide good value in terms of cargo space). For the most part, the daring athletes doing the high-wire acts went largely unnoticed by the crowd. After all, why look up when you could look down at whatever sugary snack your parents had bought you to shove into your mouth?

But my brothers were (and still are) different. They looked up at the performance high above the ground in awe and admiration. Maybe because it was (and still is) an amazing feat to walk across a small wire at an elevated height, especially before the days of high-quality safety netting; or maybe because my dad was too cheap to buy them snacks; or maybe because the high wire reminded them of the clothesline that shot out from the balcony of our grandmother's apartment in Verdun, Quebec—John and Larry became determined to duplicate the high-wire act on their next visit to Nana's.

It turns out, the third maybe was the right answer.

After returning home from the circus, pumped full of adrenalin like most kids would be after seeing gigantic exotic animals in the middle of the city, John and Larry bided their time until they could try out what they'd just seen under the big top (minus the safety net, proper equipment and years of training). As it turned out, they didn't have to wait very long. A week after their visit to the circus, my brothers found themselves at Nana's apartment. Led by Larry, the stuntman/football player/thrill-seeker of the family, my older brothers went out onto the balcony. With no balancing stick or a lick of common sense, Larry hoisted himself to the level of the clothesline. John, the sensible one, quickly realized his younger brother's mistake—but not soon enough. As Larry lost his balance (which he'd never really had), John lunged to grab his arm, and they both fell through the air with the greatest of ease. Only they were not daring young men on a flying trapeze. They were the Patterson boys on the third-floor clothesline, and they landed with a thud onto a mercifully and miraculously placed pad of grass.

Having not been there (I was still several years from actual existence at that point), I can't accurately describe what my mom's reaction must have been when she got the call from her mother telling her that my brothers had fallen from the balcony. But I imagine it must have been something along the lines of "AAAAAAAAAHHH HHHHHHHHHHHHHHHHHHHHHHHHHHHHHHHHHHHHHHH HHH!"

In the end, John had several broken ribs and Larry a broken arm. My mom's broken heart quickly turned to anger at her own mother for not paying closer attention to the boys.

Which brings me to a couple of important lessons in parenting:

1. Grandparents are fantastic, but they generally don't move very fast, and their houses are generally not kid-proofed, since their kids are generally adults. So if you're dropping your kids off at their grandparents' place, it's up to YOU, as the parent, to spot potential dangers (like clotheslines on third-floor balconies) and take necessary precautions (this could include telling your kids not to go on the balcony, locking the balcony door, and if necessary, forming a barricade to prevent access to said balcony).
2. Accidents WILL happen. With all kids. Especially rambunctious ones. You are never going to stop all mishaps, so the best you can do is try to prevent the worst ones from taking place. This is still impossible because kids don't tell you when they're about to do something stupid—they just do it.

Now by the time it got to me, son number *five*, my parents had pretty much seen all there was to see of their kids doing stupid things, so they weren't going to even try to stop me from doing them. I would learn by experience, just as my brothers had.

Like the time I tried to ski jump off our roof.

I was eight years old (prime Patterson stupidity years) and had just watched an episode of *ABC's Wide World of Sports*, which featured not only a ski-jumping competition but also the show's opening sequence where a ski jumper loses his balance while speeding down a ramp, then falls out of control at a speed no human should be going and crashes *through* a building. The accompanying voice-over talked about "the agony of defeat." Indeed.

Most rational people would see that footage and think, "Oh, my God! I am NEVER going to try ski jumping." But eight-year-old me saw it and thought, "Cool! I could do that!"

Immediately after watching the show, I rooted around our basement, found a pair of skis (cross-country, of course—downhill skis were "too goddamn expensive") and headed outside to try this new sport. Never mind that I had never skied before, or that we didn't live near a hill of any sort. I would find a way.

I surveyed the area around our house and the surrounding yard, which was snow-covered (very important), and determined that the most ramp-like thing was . . . our house. It was the quintessential shape that all children think of when they draw a house: square on the bottom, triangle on top.

So with skis in hand, I began climbing the television antenna tower that was tenuously attached to our house to prepare for ski-jump glory. I have no idea where my parents and my brothers were at the time. One nice thing about having much older siblings and parents who are "going through some things" is that you can, for the most part, spend your childhood unsupervised.

It wasn't easy climbing that antenna tower while holding skis. After all, it was certainly not designed to be used that way. But also, skis are long and eight-year-olds are not. So it took a while, using one hand to steady myself and the other to hold on to the skis.

Eventually, I made it to the roof.

What people don't tell you about roofs (unless, I imagine, you're a roofing professional or perhaps a squirrel) is that they're not the easiest surface to walk on even if you aren't carrying anything. But they are particularly precarious to small boys carrying cross-country skis.

I don't know if I took two steps or three, but I'm certain that I didn't make it to the fourth step before gravity firmly set in and I fell, backwards, off our roof.

Two things saved me that day: the fact that our house was a bungalow (so the roof wasn't very high) and the fact that the ground was covered in a generous layer of snow (something John and Larry would have benefited greatly from under Nana's balcony twenty years earlier).

I can't remember if it hurt. I can't remember if I scratched my face on the shingles on the way down. All I remember is rolling down the roof and falling into a pile of snow, then letting out a cry, which brought Dad running and shaking his head.

"Jesus Christ, Stephen! What the hell are you doing?"

"I wanted to practise ski jumping off the roof."

"Oh . . . well, you shouldn't do that. Are you okay?"

"I think so."

"Okay. Well, lunch is ready."

Back to the present day and I can't tell yet if the Patterson fool-hardiness has been passed down to my girls. But I do know that the best a dad can do is protect his children when he's with them and teach them things that should be common sense (like don't walk across clotheslines). It's a tough gig because kids' accidents happen in the microseconds between non-accidents. If they were music, those mishaps would happen on the offbeat. So does that make all jazz music an accident? You tell me.

CHAPTER 20

Take the Bully
by the Horns

When you're not being outsmarted and outnumbered by your children while simultaneously trying to protect them from each other, you will also have to do what you can to protect them from other kids.

Bullying has changed completely since I was a little boy. Especially because, as the youngest of five boys with a large older brother who was a skilled fighter, I didn't have to deal with much of it myself. I got in one fight with the schoolyard bully when I moved to London from Toronto in grade four. The fight was declared a draw (which is a loss for the bully), then we became friends and he stopped being a bully. So win-win.

What I didn't know about bullying is that kindergarten girls are also adept at it. This form is more subtle, of course, than simple fist fights, but it's no less harmful to the bullied child's psyche.

One day, Scarlett came home from school and complained that a little girl on her bus (a year older) was pushing her and calling her a baby. Which, for a four-year-old is roughly akin to an adult calling another adult an arsehole or something much worse that I won't write here because I don't want this book to be slapped with a Parental Advisory sticker (in fact, I want this to be read by parents before they have been otherwise advised). Scarlett was heartbroken because the one thing you don't want to be anymore when you're four years old is a baby. You've already been through all that baby stuff. You're growing up now. The other little girl knew exactly how to hurt Scarlett's feelings. I don't know why she was doing this, nor, frankly, did I care. Someone was making my little girl feel bad and was also pushing her. So my immediate reaction was to rectify the situation the way I had learned to deal with such things when I was a boy. But Nancy convinced me that I couldn't just call my brother Ross and ask him to fly to Ontario from Nova Scotia to beat up a little girl. So I had to come up with another idea.

We've always encouraged Scarlett to tell people, including other kids, to stop if they're doing or saying things that make her uncomfortable. This is good advice in dealing with distant aunts, uncles and cousins who, on their rare visits, try to hoist her up in the air, which is always a weird move to me. If you see a child only once or twice a year, don't make picking her up and throwing her in the air your opening move. Just because she's smaller than you doesn't mean she's a toy to be tossed around. You wouldn't do that if you met an adult jockey, would you? Well, maybe that's a bad example. Those jockeys do spend most of their time whipping horses into running against their will. Maybe they deserve to be tossed in the air a bit.

Anyway, the point is that while it's important for children to know it's okay to speak up when they're feeling uncomfortable, that isn't always effective when they are dealing with other young children. In particular, it doesn't work well with young bullies who might not even know they're being bullies (or maybe they're just tiny arsehole versions of their arsehole parents, who never had their own behaviour corrected as children). So I sat down with Scarlett and came up with some responses to the taunts she was receiving. I explained that sometimes bullies are just mad because they don't have friends, and it's always better to be friends with people than enemies. And since one way to make new friends is to make them laugh, we decided to come up with a witty comeback.

The next time the little girl called Scarlett a baby, my daughter responded, "Thanks! People LOVE babies!" and smiled. It froze the bully in her tracks. I'm not sure if she actually smiled (bullies are often not quite bright enough to comprehend repartee), but she and Scarlett eventually became friends, which was a proud moment for my daughter. And to be honest, a pretty proud dad moment for me too.

Still, sometimes you have to deal with bullies the old-fashioned way.

Like the time Scarlett and I were at the local playground, where lots of the neighbourhood kids go. Most of the kids know each other, but there are always a few new faces. On this particular day, there were a handful of kids around, including one rather large boy who may have been five or fifteen. This oversized "little guy" had declared himself king of the castle and was standing at the top of one of the slides, not letting other kids go down or come up. Now, I know kids are not technically supposed to go *up* slides, but if you always abide by the rules, you'll always be letting the man keep you down . . . man.

Anyway, as several little children tried to get to the top of the slide, this little-big bully would put out his arm to stop them. He wasn't punching or hitting, but he *was* pushing. Some of the kids were starting to cry. I was getting ready to intervene—I intended to politely ask the little shit if he wouldn't mind letting some of the other kids on the slide—when Scarlett took it upon herself to step in. She approached stealthily from behind the bully, keeping low to the ground (the default position for a four-year-old). Then when he was looking the other way, pushing other kids, she calmly but firmly kicked him in the arse. As a matter of fact, she kicked him in the arse hard enough that he FLEW over the slide and beyond the kids he had been pushing, landing face first in some wood chips on the ground. The other children cheered as they made their way to the top of the slide. The little bully, unhurt except for his pride, started to cry, making the wood chips he had landed in stick to his face.

His mother, who had been sitting on a bench looking at her phone, oblivious to everything, looked up and asked, "What happened?"

The bully pointed at sweet little Scarlett at the bottom of the slide and said, "She kicked me!"

The mom looked at Scarlett's smiling face and then at mine, realized the similarities, and said, "Your daughter pushed my son!"

To which I happily replied, "I don't mind."

It was a lovely moment for all of us. Except the bully and his mom. Which somehow made it even lovelier.

Now, I'm not saying that all confrontations with bullies can be solved with a quick-witted line or an even quicker kick to the arse. As kids grow older, they grow more sophisticated, and sadly these days, the bullies don't have to step away from their computers or phones to do the bullying. They do it anonymously online—the most cowardly type of bullying there is.

I didn't realize we would have to start teaching Scarlett to deal with bullies as early as kindergarten. I was hoping she wouldn't know what bullies were for at least a few more years yet. But in reality, bullying starts early, and if it's not stopped in its tracks, it gets worse. So even though I'm a dad who grew up the youngest of five sons and am now raising two daughters, I'm going to make damn sure my girls learn the lessons that my dad taught me:

1. Don't be an arsehole to others.
2. Don't start fights, but know how to finish them. And do it with repartee, wherever possible. Or a firm kick to the arse when absolutely necessary.

And the third lesson is the one Scarlett taught me, that playground bully and hopefully his mom that day: never underestimate a little girl with a big smile and an even bigger kick.

CHAPTER 21

The Baby Lioness

So far in her young life, Norah has not been bullied. I believe this will continue to be the case because, as a Leo, she is already exhibiting lion-like qualities.

As Norah's parents, we have been very patient. After all, we had excellent training during Scarlett's babyhood. Also, Scarlett, for the most part, has been a very caring big sister who understands that Norah is a baby and doesn't know what she's doing when she grabs our hair, sticks her fingers in our eyes, or in my case, rips my reading glasses off my face and throws them to the floor at every possible opportunity.

Scarlett might believe this is just normal baby behaviour. But I'm not so sure.

Is Norah just being a baby, or is she going completely alpha to establish her dominance over our household? I mean, who rips reading glasses off someone's face, throws them on the floor, then smiles as if to say, "What are you going to do about it?" Who grasps a cup of water, looks at you, and when you say, "Don't throw that!" laughs like a maniac and gleefully chucks it at your face? Who goes up to someone who is sitting down, minding his own business, and punches him right in the testicles?

Sure, she technically can't form a fist or make a punching motion (yet), plus as far as I know, she is unaware of the male anatomy (which, if I have my way, will remain the case well into her twenties). But honestly, I sometimes think that Norah knows *exactly* what she is doing and is enjoying all the "she doesn't know what she's doing" time that she can. Sure, she's playing. But it's a power play for control of the house.

To be fair, as I write this, Norah is teething, which, if I were going through it, would probably make me want to punch people in the testicles too. Of all the baffling things in human development, the way that teeth come in has to be the most inexplicable (and painful). Imagine you're a baby with nice soft gums that you have just gotten used to smacking together to make a percussive sound that only you can truly appreciate. Then suddenly, those gum-drums of yours are penetrated by sharp projectiles that are apparently shooting up from INSIDE your own mouth, and by the way, are attached to you now. That's not anatomy—that's a horror movie! So babies react in the way we all would in the face of such a terrifying situation: they scream at the top of their lungs! As a parent, you try to console your screaming baby by holding her close to you and reassuring her that it's going to be okay. But your baby is understandably skeptical about that, because those arsehole teeth just keep coming in! As this drags on (for weeks and months, in fact), neither you nor your baby is actually sure things are ever going to be okay again.

This likely explains why Norah's favourite thing to do while she is teething and I'm trying to console her is to put her hands in my mouth and try to rip my own teeth out. I keep telling myself she's doing this because she believes she is saving me from pain—sort of a "Dad, those are the things that are attacking me from the inside! Let me rip those out for you and then you get mine out of me, okay?" But the defiant expression on her face sometimes tells a different story. The look seems to say, "it's going to be okay, is it? Does THIS feel okay, old man? Huh? Does that feel okay to you?" Then she yanks on my front teeth like she's a middle-aged dad trying to perform a proper chin-up for the first time in his life.

So yes, teething is tough and pretty much any behaviour a baby exhibits during this time can probably be chalked up to the pain and discomfort she's going through. This is especially true when the teeth make their grand entrance while the baby is *sleeping*. Imagine if you were woken up by the pain of something stabbing you from inside your own mouth. You'd be pissed off and looking for someone— anyone—to attack. Which is especially bad news if you're that baby's mother and are sleeping beside her, with the main food source so temptingly close to her face.

Nancy has tried to explain to me what it's like to be bitten on the nipple by a baby with new teeth, and while her explanations have been eloquent, I'm sure I still don't quite comprehend it. For Norah, it's simply a matter of getting used to these new body parts that have entered her life so painfully (and rudely). She does this by chomping down on a body part that is not hers but is very familiar to her. Compared to this, an accidental punch by a baby's tiny hand to my (average-sized, I think) testicles is really nothing. Well, I mean it's not "nothing," but I can't try to tell Nancy it's in the same ballpark. Pun intended.

So teething babies get a pass on behaviour we wouldn't tolerate from any adult or even any toddler with a full set of teeth. But I'm still not sure Norah isn't milking this moment like, well, a baby chomping on a boob to get milk.

For instance, in addition to ripping the glasses off my face whenever they are within range of her tiny arm, Norah has also recently taken to ripping the remaining hairs out of the top of my head when I put her on my shoulders. She does this while screaming with delight (it's a different scream than the teething scream, because she's laughing while she does it). She has also taken to straight-arming me and Nancy like a Hall of Fame running back avoiding a tackle whenever she doesn't want to go to sleep—which is always, because she *never* wants to go to sleep. In fact, sometimes she will lull me into thinking she's almost asleep and then rouse herself to get away by pushing off me like she's doing a backwards dive off a high cliff. This makes me hold on to her even tighter so she doesn't dive head first into the floor, and then she responds by screaming out with the common baby call of "Mamamamamamamamamamamama," which roughly translates to "Mother! This idiot is trying to put me to sleep. I'm not ready for sleep, obviously! It's almost time for *Saturday Night Live*!"

The moment Nancy comes into the room, Norah basically jumps into her arms, smiles at me as if to say, "I told you she would come," and stops screaming. Experts say this is because babies need their mothers much more than their fathers, especially when they're teething. Those same experts also say, "She doesn't mean anything by it—she's just a baby." But I can tell by the look in her eyes that this kid is playing me like a fiddle. And not the foot-stamping, hand-clapping, joy-filled fiddle you would hear on Canada's East Coast. I mean like an out-of-tune, ominous fiddle from a horror movie soundtrack.

So sometimes, when Nancy can't see or hear me, I will get right into baby Norah's face and shout-whisper into her tiny ear, "Hey! I'm your dad. You're a baby. You *have* to listen to me!"

And she will respond by ripping my glasses off my face and laughing like a maniac.

Nancy and Scarlett laugh about something while Norah dreams of the next time she'll rip the glasses off my face.
(Photo credit: John Hryniuk.)

CHAPTER 22

And Sometimes You Have to Suck Snot Out

If you've heard the expression "snot-nosed kid" before, it was probably being used by an older person to describe a young adult. For example, it's how a man who has worked at a company for two or three decades might describe a new employee who has only been alive for two or three decades and comes in with newfangled ideas, like sending text messages instead of telegrams.

But once you have young children of your own, you realize that snot-nosed kids are actual beings: they have noses, and those noses are often full of snot. This is especially true when those kids are babies and have no idea how to get the snot out of their noses themselves. Although I learned this with Scarlett, it's something I had pushed to the very back of my mind and almost forgotten about until I had a visceral reminder when Norah was just a few months old.

SOMETIMES PARENTS SUCK THE SNOT OUT OF THEIR BABY'S NOSE.

I would repeat that, but then you might not be able to forget it.

One night, Norah was heavily congested, as babies sometimes get. That means they can't sleep because they can't breathe, which means you can't sleep either, even though you are breathing just fine. Or more specifically, it means your wife, who is lying on the floor directly beside your baby because the crib is too far away from the bed, can't sleep. And you, being the hero you are, are sleeping comfortably beside your five-year-old in a bedroom downstairs, both of you snoring happily.

The guilt of being comfortable as your spouse struggles to tend to your baby is powerful. If you're not a Catholic, it's the most powerful guilt there is. On this occasion, I was awoken at 4:30 a.m. to a strange suction sound emanating from our bedroom. To the untrained ear, it sounded like an alien had broken into the house and was currently sucking my spouse's brain out through the top of her head. Or perhaps it was sucking out our baby daughter's brain, since she was screaming loudly enough for her displeasure to be heard by life forms on all other planets in the solar system.

Naturally, you do what any caring spouse/protective father would: you try to sleep through the racket, hoping that it will soon stop. After what might seem like a full hour of brain-sucking shrieking (but was more likely about three minutes), you'll probably realize that the aliens are not going to stop. So you'll stumble into the room and come upon a sight that no parenting book can ever prepare you for: your wife with one end of a tube in her mouth and the other end inserted into your baby daughter's nose. In many ways, it would have been a less strange sight if it *were* an alien.

Then your wife, the ever-helpful play-by-play commentator, explains what is happening: "She's really congested, so I'm sucking the boogers out of her nose."

It's one of those sentences you never imagined any human being saying, let alone your beloved wife in reference to your beloved off-spring. So it takes a moment before you can respond with a sleep-deprived "Yes, I see that. Um, did you get one?"

That's another sentence you never thought you'd say, at least in reference to the pursuit of an ever-elusive booger. But you *did* say it, so now your wife must respond with proof of her booger-sucking prowess and an invitation that there's no way you can decline without upsetting your marital harmony.

"Yes! Come and see!"

And that's how I found myself shuffling reluctantly towards my deranged snot-sucking spouse and my still-squealing baby girl in order to verify something that I didn't want to look at.

"THAT WAS *ALL* IN HER NOSE!" Nancy said proudly, displaying a tube very nearly full of a substance no human eyes are supposed to see. "No wonder she couldn't breathe, eh?"

I didn't reply at first because I had to fight the sick feeling that was forming in my throat. My wife was looking at me with the same proud expression Scarlett had when she insisted that I see the first forty or fifty poops she had "made" in the toilet all by herself. So after a big swallow that protected us all, I found my voice and said, "Yeah, that's enough to stop anyone from breathing. And you just . . . sucked it right out, eh?"

"I did! Here, go rinse this out for me!"

Now, if you've ever been handed something disgusting, you know it's not a very good feeling. Dirty diapers are disgusting. Bags of dog poop are equally or even MORE disgusting (because those bags often aren't made specifically for poop collection). Your coping mechanism is likely to get rid of the offending thing as soon as possible. That explains the speed with which dog owners dash to the nearest trash can and new parents make a beeline to the life-saving and odour-blocking Diaper Genie. (Robin Williams as Genie from *Aladdin* wouldn't have been nearly as cheery if he'd been locked in THERE for ten thousand years). Yet when you are handed a vial of snot that came from the nasal cavity of your adorable baby and was sucked out by the woman you've spent a good deal of time kissing on the mouth, a lot of things run through your mind:

1. Did she SWALLOW any of our baby's boogers?
2. Is this the grossest thing she has ever swallowed? And if not, should I immediately have my stomach pumped?
3. . . .

Okay, I guess it's just the two things, really.

But the moral of all this, if there is one, is that there is no end to what a loving parent (most likely a loving mom) will do to relieve her baby's suffering.

And while I have so far (knock on wood) managed to avoid becoming a member of the baby-booger suckers, I grudgingly admire these people for their devotion to the craft.

CHAPTER 23

This Is Going to Hurt Me More Than It Hurts You

Any parent who has ever heard his or her child cry out in pain (which is every parent) knows that the old adage "This is going to hurt me more than it hurts you" is actually strangely true. The sound of your child in pain cuts through any other sound in any environment. Whether it's a teething baby wailing in the middle of the night or a toddler coming to you with the news that another kid is pushing them around in the schoolyard (I still wish I could bring in my brother Ross on these occasions), you feel it in your guts every time.

Of course, children cry out in pain only when they know there is someone around who can actually hear them, which is usually one or both of their parents. Otherwise, what's the point? Crying is a child's built-in ambulance siren. It lets you know that she needs help *now*. So she turns it on when there's a parent in range (the range is pretty large because that siren can get very loud), and it signals that others should get out of the way because this is an EMERGENCY. In certain instances, a grandparent or favourite uncle, aunt, or family friend may also get the siren. But if none of these people are around to hear, it's amazing how much a child's pain threshold goes up.

In times of feigned injury, it's easy to call bullshit on your child by . . . well, literally calling "Bullshit!" like my dad used to do with me. Or perhaps you prefer to paraphrase slightly with "You're not hurt." And sometimes, the most effective way to deal with your child's perceived pain is to not react at all until the pain miraculously disappears.

When a child is truly hurting, though, that's when your own heart takes a bit of a beating. I know I'm in for a long line of dealing with heartbreak with Scarlett, who has the blessing and curse of being a truly empathetic individual. The empathy I have for her she has for pretty much *everyone* she knows. She doesn't want anyone to feel pain ever and she doesn't understand when others are mean to her or any of her friends. Nancy is the same way so sometimes it's up to me to teach them how not to give a shit about people who aren't worth it.

Case in point: Scarlett was upset over a little boy in her class who didn't want to sit beside her at lunch. Apparently when she sat down beside him, he would get up and leave. If she followed him to a new seat, he would move again. It upset her that he didn't want to sit beside her. She wondered why he didn't like her. So I had to explain that sometimes people just need their own space (when Mommy or Daddy is going to the bathroom, for instance), and that it didn't mean he didn't like her. Then she explained to me that the little boy had actually said, "I don't like you." "Well, then, my love, he's not worth it," I said. "Because anyone who doesn't like you isn't worth liking." This was a strange concept to Scarlett. I told her that it's nice to have friends—and she has lots of them—but sometimes there are people who won't want to be her friend at a particular moment, and there's no use wasting her time trying to befriend them. This was much better advice, in my opinion, than blurting out my original thought, which was, "Who cares about him? He's obviously an arsehole."

I don't want to teach my little girls that they shouldn't care about people or want to make new friends. I just need them to know that some people aren't worth the effort. The fact that this is such a difficult concept to communicate to Scarlett is proof of how caring and empathetic she really is. As for our little lioness, Norah, I feel like it's going to be an easier concept to convey to her. I say this because the other day, when I was trying to playfully withhold some food from her, she stared at me with an expression that said, "Old man, if you don't give me that right now, I will eat YOU." That kid's going to be alright.

Sisters happy together. My main goal in life is to keep them that way.

The point is that being a parent to young children is often painful—whether you're trying to teach them something you don't fully comprehend yourself, consoling them when they seem inconsolable or just trying to physically keep up with them. In the course of helping your children "find their legs" in various activities, you're going to hurt your own knees. And your back. And your neck. And every other part of your body. This is especially true when your infant learns to jump on your lap and doesn't understand that your testicles aren't a trampoline (or fully understands but jumps on them anyway).

Still, despite all the exhausting, nauseating, heartbreaking and physically excruciating moments, you'll continue to do everything you can to be the perfect parent. But just remember this one important thing: you never will be.

There's no such thing as a perfect parent because there's no such thing as a perfect child (yes, even YOURS). All you can really do is take what your imperfect parents taught you as a child and pass that on to your children, then pray that they vastly improve on it.

Good talk.

CHAPTER 24

My Food Is Mocking Me

Your child will eventually move beyond breastfeeding to solid foods. Opinions vary as to exactly when that should happen. But a good guideline to follow is that if your child asks, "Excuse me, could I trouble you for some breastmilk, please, Mommy?" then it's pretty close to quitting time. (Note: For affluent British children, these could in fact be their first spoken words.)

The day that children start to eat non-breast-milk foods is the day they start to rebel against those foods and exhibit their own free will over menu choices. As a parent, I marvel at this stage of human cognitive development because when I was a small child, it sure as hell wasn't an option for me. Back in those days, there was Gerber baby food and that was it. There was no such thing as artisanal foods for small children. The term "organic" was assumed to be a misspelling of "orgasmic" (so a sign for "organic" tomatoes would have led to some very confused shoppers headed home for some very messy experimentation).

I have a vague memory of my mom feeding me some sort of mushy food, which apparently I ate enthusiastically because she later told me that my older brothers used to bring their friends over to see how much food I could devour in a single sitting. Every entertainer has a unique origin story.

What I remember VERY clearly, though, is that whatever food was put in front of me by my dad, I was expected to eat. There was no thought whatsoever of me saying, "I don't like this!" and no option of any sort of meal substitution. "Oh, you don't like it, Stephen?" my dad might have said in an alternate universe. "Terribly sorry. Let me bring back the menu for you to peruse again."

This also went for food that was prepared incorrectly.

When pancakes were left in the griddle too long and turned out charcoal black instead of golden brown, we were still expected to eat them. Fortunately, as a Canadian kid, this wasn't tough to do because of the vast quantity and quality of 100% Canadian maple syrup available. With enough of that sweet nectar poured on any burnt pancake, waffle, or if necessary, actual brick of charcoal, we could choke it down. Also, I'm not sure if we got all this syrup salvation from the maple tree in our front yard, but knowing how cheap my dad is, I have no doubt he tried to tap it.

Barbecuing was a particularly perplexing challenge at our house. My dad's barbecue of choice was the same model used by the cavemen who first discovered fire. Plus, Slim liked his steaks well done, which is a polite way to say burnt to a leather-like consistency, and then cooked for another five minutes. I assume this was handed down from Dad's dad, who probably cooked the same way. It would have gone unchecked indefinitely if not for the intervention of my stepmother, Barb.

Barb came into my life when I was around eleven years old, a few years after my parents had split and about a year after I'd moved with my dad and Ross to London. To say that Barb's culinary skills were a step up from what I had experienced before would be a gross understatement. How gross? Almost as gross as a burnt pancake with no maple syrup.

Before Barb came on the scene, I ate vast quantities of meat and potatoes. But she introduced new foods like fish, chicken and things called vegetables. It was a new experience for me to discover that salads (1) existed, (2) were good for you and (3) could actually taste DELICIOUS. This was especially true for me when the salads included tomatoes. (But not the organic kind. That would have made for an awkward family dinner.)

For some reason, I liked tomatoes instantly. Maybe it was because Barb usually served them with balsamic vinegar and salt, or maybe it was because Dad actually grew them himself in the backyard. Of course, Slim gardened a bit differently than most other gardeners. Instead of using purpose-made trellises to support the tomato plants, for example, he used hockey sticks, many of which my brothers and I had thought we were still using. So when the summertime road hockey season commenced for most young Canadian boys, the Pattersons had to sit it out because our dad was growing tomatoes. It was a confusing concept to all but our Italian neighbours, whose fathers were also using their hockey sticks to garden. Our Italian friends would turn to playing soccer, but my brothers and I thought they were crazy for playing foot hockey, where body checking wasn't even allowed.

Nowadays, people talk about "eating local" and "from farm to table" as a way of supporting community farmers, fighting inflationary prices and even addressing climate change. When you grow your own vegetables in your own backyard, you can't get much more local than that. You know *exactly* where those veggies have been because you've been watching them grow the whole time. And as my dad always liked to point out, "When you grow it yourself, they can't put a goddamn tax on it." Most importantly, though, when the growing season was over and my brothers and I were reunited with our hockey sticks, we knew they had served a higher purpose. Also, we could blame our bad shots on the fact that the stick blades had been buried in fertilizer for a good portion of the year.

Dad still likes to grow his own vegetables, which is weird because he doesn't like to eat vegetables at all. I guess this is also a good time to point out that my dad has no taste. Not in the sense of knowing which things go together to make the best outfits or food-and-wine pairings (though he's not great at those things either). No, I mean he literally can't taste things. I'm not sure how it happened, but it does explain a lot. Suffice it to say that you don't want the person making the meals at your house to have no functioning taste buds. This person should be able to at least taste the difference between sponge cake and an actual sponge.

Nowhere was this more apparent than with school lunches.

My dad's approach to school lunch was the same as his overall approach to life: find the least expensive option and continue with that option indefinitely. For me, this meant a mysterious meat called mock chicken. If you've never heard of it, you're extremely lucky and probably in better health than I am. If you have heard of it—and especially if you've actually *eaten* it once or twice—you may shudder slightly at the memory, smile knowingly and then move on with your life. But if you grew up on mock-chicken school lunches . . . well, you poor, poor bastard. You are my people.

Mock chicken was (and I understand still is!) the cheapest lunch-meat available. This is because it's made of ingredients that don't really cost anything because they're not really real. If you're looking for it at the deli counter, you're not at a very high-quality deli. Mock chicken has only one distinguishable quality, and it isn't the colour of the meat itself, which is a colour no one would choose in a meat they have plans to eat. Grey would be a substantial upgrade. But the marketing gurus behind mock chicken (damn them all to hell) did something ingenious that no one else in the meat industry had thought of: they coloured the outer edge of the meat . . . ORANGE! My dad took one look at the price of mock chicken and nodded his head approvingly. He might have been thrown briefly by its questionable hue, but no doubt he rebounded when he saw the orange outer ring and thought, "Orange! The colour of . . . oranges. Those are full of vitamin C! This nutritious meat is a steal!"

So began my unfortunate relationship with this mysterious meat.

Dad made me mock-chicken sandwiches for lunch pretty much every day of my elementary school life. At first I tried to trade lunches like all the other kids seemed to be doing, but I gave up after a couple of weeks when not a single classmate would take the bait. In fairness, it's tough to trade something when you really don't know what it is. A typical attempt at a mock-chicken lunch trade went something like this:

Other kid: Hey, Steve, wanna trade lunches?
Me: SURE!!!!
Other kid: Well, what have you got?
Me: It's . . . um, mock chicken.
Other kid: What's that?

Me: Well, it's sort of like chicken. Except it's not.

Other kid (looking at my lunch): Why is it orange on the outside?

Me: My dad says that's the vitamin C.

Other kid: Hmm. That doesn't look very good. And why is there a hockey puck in your lunch?

Me: That's not a hockey puck. My dad baked cookies!

Other kid: Oh. I think I'll just stick to my own lunch.

Me: Probably a smart move.

I had resigned myself to having mock chicken every lunchtime for the rest of my life until a twist of fate (actually a medical order) changed everything. Apparently, all the artificial ingredients in the mock meat had played havoc with my stomach and eventually resulted in me coming home from school sick. So my dad took me to the doctor, and he actually said, "Stop feeding your son mock chicken." I'm not sure he'd ever had to give that as a medical order before—or, I assume, since.

So my dad had a decision to make: he could move up the lunch-meat food chain to the next least expensive option (bologna), or he could prepare sandwiches with real meat, like my best friend Ted's mom did. (Every sandwich Ted brought to school looked like it had been prepared at a professional delicatessen.) Instead, my dad landed on a third option no other parent had thought of: he abandoned sandwiches completely and went straight to soup.

Dad wasn't adept at making soup, but he found one recipe that he could prepare quickly, cheaply and in vast quantities, and he went with that: split-pea soup. For those who might want to try this at home, let's see if I can walk you through it: you take a bunch of dried peas and throw them in boiling water, and when they split, it's ready. Split-pea soup. It's just as delicious as it sounds.

Dad would make vast quantities of split-pea soup, then store them in old margarine containers that we used because proper Tupperware was "TOO GODDAMN EXPENSIVE, STEPHEN!" (As was real butter, apparently.) Then he would take the old margarine containers full of new split-pea soup and stack them in our fridge and our freezer, since each batch yielded many, many servings. More often than not, he would give me a margarine container straight from the freezer so that I ended up going to school with a frozen solid block. My dad somehow believed this frozen block of soup, straight out of the freezer in the morning, would magically transform itself into a piping hot bowl of deliciousness by lunchtime.

Some astute young readers may take this time to ask, "What's the big deal, Steve? You could just put it in the microwave, right?" Well, right, I guess. If our school had had a microwave, which it did not. My only option was to bring the soup into class with me and sit on it like a mother hen. I desperately hoped my body heat would be enough to thaw it out by lunch. I also remember . . . um, how do I put this? Well, on more than one occasion, I would fart. Because I had learned, even by grade four, that a human fart has an exit temperature of about 98.6°F (that's 37°C, if you must know). That could be the difference between my soup thawing or not thawing, which frankly was more important to me than preserving social graces in grade four.

In short, I wasn't a very fun kid to sit beside.

But no matter what I did, my efforts usually came up flat(ulent). At lunch, I resigned myself to eating cold and sometimes semi-frozen soup, which was somehow even tougher to trade than a mock-chicken sandwich.

Me: Hey, you want to trade lunches?

Other kid: Um, it's not mock chicken, is it?

Me: No, not anymore. I've got soup!

Other kid: Soup? Are you sick? Is it chicken noodle?

Me: No, I'm fine . . . well, relatively fine. It's cold split-pea soup!

Other: Cold soup? No, thanks!

Me: Why not? Have you ever tried it?

Other: No, but I know that I barely like soup when it's hot. So I definitely won't like it cold. See ya later!

And with that, the kid would run away, probably to warn my other classmates that I was going to try to trade them my cold soup for literally anything else.

The nice thing about underwhelming your kids on a daily basis is how easily they might be amazed one day from a break in routine. In fact, it could lead to one of the best days of their young lives. It was a sunny day in May 1980. I opened my lunch bag, fully expecting the usual unremarkable sight of split peas stuck between tiny pieces of ice (or if I had been particularly gassy that morning, floating in water). But on this magical May day, my mayday was answered: I was met with what would have been an unremarkable and perhaps even disappointing sight for any other kid, but for me was an absolute miracle. "YES!" I exclaimed. "MARGARINE!"

My dad had screwed up. He had sent me off to school with a margarine container that contained actual margarine. And since we had already used it to spread on toast that morning, the magical margarine had some bonus breadcrumbs in it (or as I like to think of them, poor people's croutons). I happily ate the whole tub and honestly can't remember if I was sick afterwards. But even if I was, it was still better than eating mock chicken or split-pea soupsicles.

All of this to say, you don't have to feed your children filet mignon or organic foods every meal to be a good dad. But there is something to the expression "You are what you eat." And the better the ingredients you put into your kids' lunches, the better your kids will feel and the better their chances of becoming the best they can be. So while I am still partially composed of questionable food from my childhood, I guarantee that my daughters are already made up of better stuff, which is why they are already better people than me.

CHAPTER 25

Meal Time Is Real Time

As I mentioned earlier, when I was eleven years old my stepmom, Barb, stepped into the role of making my lunches and dinners. From that point on, things improved dramatically. I found Barb's cooking to be delicious and I would always let her know because she appreciated the appreciation.

The one exception was ham.

I don't like ham (with or without green eggs). I never have and I never will. (Which is weird because I like bacon and other types of pork.) But Barb will never know this. This is because the first time she made ham for me, she described it as her specialty. I was very excited because I liked everything else she had made so much! And then she put pineapple on top, which apparently some people love, but I dislike pineapple about as much as I dislike ham.

I remember the battle that went on inside my head when I took my first bite of ham and pineapple together, hoping two dislikes would equal one like. As I looked across the table at Barb, who was watching me expectantly, I had to fight the urge to spit the gross combination across the room like someone who had taken a swig of a beer only to find out the bottle had been used as an ashtray. Barb asked, "Well? What do you think?" And I replied, in what is still one of my finest acting performances, "Mmmmmmmmmmm. It is *soooooooooo* good!" I lied right to her face. I acted like ham and pineapple were my favourite foods when in fact they were (and still are) my least favourites.

I remember whispering to my dad, "I don't like this," and him giving me the glare (if the glare is strong enough, the child just understands that it's time to stop talking).

I never did tell Barb that I didn't like ham, so she continued to make it for us for every holiday meal and special occasion. And every single time it was served, I told her how delicious it was, which made both her and my dad smile, but for very different reasons.

Fast-forward now to young Scarlett eating her first meals. It's a very different experience from my childhood. For one, Nancy is a good cook and is very health-conscious. The foods Scarlett gets are better than my early meals of well-done steaks and blackened pancakes. But the other important difference is that unlike young me, Scarlett doesn't think she *has* to eat anything. I truly believed that Slim would have let me starve to death if I hadn't eaten what was put in front of me. No matter how much I try to channel my inner Slim and encourage her to eat her food, Scarlett calls my bluff every time. Also, she is a little girl with a small appetite. I've never been either of those things.

The first time I attempted to feed Scarlett, I remember taking a spoonful of whatever it was (it was a purée, so there's really no telling— I just know it wasn't mock chicken) and trying to shovel it into her mouth. Nancy quickly corrected me and pointed out that Scarlett ate in small quantities a number of times throughout the day. The next time I tried to feed her, I decided to share Scarlett's food as a bonding experience, and I discovered that this new baby stuff was actually pretty good. So I ended up eating most of my daughter's dinner, which made her cry because she was hungry.

Scarlett has since developed her own likes and dislikes, foodwise. Unlike me with the whole ham thing, she is *not* afraid to state her opinion. She likes steak (prepared medium rare), spaghetti with Nancy's family recipe sauce (carrots are cleverly concealed) and any dish that includes vegetables grown in our garden (which she picks herself). She will *not* eat hamburgers in large buns or fish that she knows are fish (Nancy has managed to sneak in some organic fish sticks that look like chicken fingers). And she is the only human being I know of, other than me, who doesn't like the taste of chocolate.

Nancy is amazing about including Scarlett's favourite foods in her school lunches. She prepares warm meals consisting of meat and vegetables and sometimes even Rice Krispie squares for dessert. ARE YOU KIDDING ME? RICE KRISPIE SQUARES?! Those were goddamn birthday presents to me growing up! (But of course, I want Scarlett to have it better than I did. So this is a good thing.)

There are still battles to be waged when Scarlett won't eat something that she swears she doesn't like, even though she has eaten it on several previous occasions—like mild Italian sausage, for example. Then again, Scarlett is smarter than me, so maybe Italian sausage is simply her ham and pineapple, and she has figured out at the age of five how to avoid it rather than live a culinary lie.

We're fortunate that Scarlett is a good eater for the most part. This means that she eats most of what is put in front of her—when we feed it to her. Even though Scarlett is well and fully versed in how to use forks, spoons and her personal favourite, the spork, more often than not I end up feeding her after I have finished my own meal. This is because she's a non-stop storyteller, entertaining us with tall tales of her vast adventures—many of which occurred in her other life, before she "chose" to come to us. Telling these stories requires a lot of hand gestures and that often interferes with the act of eating. Truly if I didn't feed this kid at the dinner table, she wouldn't eat. "No time, Dad! Too many stories to tell!"

Unlike her mother, Scarlett shares her spaghetti with me.

Norah, on the other hand, is the complete opposite. While Scarlett has inherited my storytelling inclination, Norah, perhaps because she isn't using words yet, gives her food her undivided attention. Any food at any time. And for the sake of efficiency, she has eliminated the middle man and eats things with her hands. As a matter of fact, if you try to introduce a plastic utensil into the process, she will grab it from your hand and throw it as far as she can—usually to the floor but sometimes as far as the wall behind her high chair. Why not? She knows someone will pick it up.

The way Norah eats as an infant reminds me of how my brothers and I ate growing up: wolf everything down as fast as you can because this may be the last food you ever get! Of course, it helps that Nancy goes out of her way to provide Norah with good food with real ingredients, rather than the processed stuff I had to be rescued from. It also helps that at every meal, our baby is surrounded by her always-attentive mom, a big sister who *loves* to entertain and a dad she has wrapped so tightly around her tiny little fingers she probably thinks of him more as a piece of jewellery than as a father-figure at this point.

Whatever the case, mealtime in our house provides some of our best family moments. No matter what the food is like (okay, it's better if the food is good), family mealtime is when you really bond. It's when your five-year-old tells you the stories about her day (and the days before she was born), when your baby discovers new tastes and sets new records for food tossing, and when your exhausted spouse gets to sit down to eat, though never, it seems, for the entire meal. (After all, your children wouldn't be doing their jobs if they allowed their mother to eat a full meal.) As kids grow older, things can get a little tense at mealtimes (I remember my brother Larry used to eat all his food while my mom was saying grace, which would make my dad yell, "GODDAMMIT, LARRY! YOUR MOTHER IS SAYING GODDAMN GRACE!"). But eating with your family at home, especially when the meal has been perfectly prepared by a proud parent (Nancy has refined my barbecuing skills to the point where my girls won't grow up thinking all meat should be crunchy), is where lasting memories come from. Even if you do have to lie for your entire life about liking ham.

CHAPTER 26

Dad-deas for Parents of Toddlers

When you grow up in a frugal household, you learn a few things about saving money. Unfortunately, frugal parents are often seen as somehow inferior to free-wheeling, big-spending parents. But in my opinion, there is nothing wrong with being frugal (except when it comes to lunches).

I don't think that I'm the best parent in my neighbourhood. In fact, of the two parents who reside in our house, I am a distant second when it comes to meal preparation, first aid, reading (French) stories, proper hygiene of distinctly female body parts, arts-and-crafts assistance, homework assistance, being home and being mommy. That said, I *am* the go-to parent when it comes to running around and playing while waiting for the school bus, playing inside games (including ball toss, which apparently some parents don't think of as an inside game), playing any game that requires a "patient" to lie down motionless (Nancy hates when I do this, but if you can fit a nap into playtime, there is nothing else I can teach you), reading (English) stories and just being daddy.

Not that parenting is a competition. We've all met overly competitive parents, and while they may appear to be terrible people on the surface, once you get to know them better, you may come to realize that they are not as terrible as you first thought. They are much worse.

In any case, there's no point in trying to out-parent other parents. Nancy and I are fortunate to have many amazing parents in our neighbourhood, which really takes the pressure off me. I realize I don't have to do everything perfectly, or even come close. I know my parenting limitations and have come to accept them. So I've devised a few parental tips that might help to make up for any daddy shortcomings you have. These "dad-deas" will go a long way to entertaining a small child throughout the many, many hours that you used to watch sports pre-fatherhood.

Here are a few of my favourites:

Food at the park. If you want your child to have food at the park but don't want to prepare said food, just go without and sidle up to one of the very prepared parents (every neighbourhood has them). This person has always got good healthy snacks. Sure, this means your child's food choices are now at the whim of the prepared parent's tastes, but it also means that your child can't be a picky eater. Win-win. (Note: You'll have to rotate parks and prepared parents for this to work over the long run.)

In lieu of toys, get boxes and bubble wrap. We received something that was shipped in a large box once, and rather than recycling it (like a good citizen SHOULD!), we decorated the box and rolled the bubble wrap down a hallway. It was a good three months of toddler bliss (though you'll need a room in the house where it's not a problem to "live around" a giant box for months at a time).

Have relatives with slightly older children. I guess this isn't really one you can plan. But my wife's sister, Chantal; her sister-in-law, Marisol; and Scarlett's older cousins Madeleine and Lila are the greatest providers of free clothes since my older brothers. The important difference is that their clothes are nice. The females in our family have impeccable taste, and they're always buying new things for their still-growing kids. Once the girls grow out of things, they make their way to us, which is perfect because new clothes for small girls come with big prices.

Don't buy a lot of new clothes. Even if you have a great supply of second-hand clothes, your child will need some new things. But the more she can wear hand-me-downs, the better. And I say this as a kid who wore his older brothers' clothes until I had to get a school uniform in high school. When your little one is a toddler, new clothes will fit her for anywhere between one hour and one-quarter of a year. New clothes aren't worth it. So if you aren't fortunate enough to have stylish family members, there are plenty of second-hand clothing stores with lots of good stuff. And if you feel too proud to visit a thrift shop, just remember that teens are now buying new jeans with rips in the knees and the arse. If you're going to look stupid anyway, you might as well save a few bucks.

Teach your toddler to spend most of her time in her bare feet. Most toddlers like nothing more than running around in bare feet, and they can escape any form of footwear with the skill of Houdini in a straightjacket. Don't fight this. Toddler shoes are the biggest consumer rip-off of all toddler clothing. They're the movie popcorn of toddler clothes. For the amount of raw material that goes into them, there's a retail markup of about 1,000 percent, and your child will grow out of them in no time. (The most I have ever eaten of a jumbo bag of movie popcorn is about one-tenth. When the butter runs out, the popcorn gets ice cold and all the space between my teeth becomes kernel storage units. That stuff should come with its own dental floss. Someone should write that idea down.) We bought Scarlett a pair of running shoes to take to preschool as backup footwear and then forgot about them. Once we remembered where they were, she had already outgrown them. So don't give in to the hype of buying new shoes for toddlers. Find someone in your neighbourhood selling shoes they don't need anymore. Trust me, they're HARDLY USED.

Remember that libraries still exist. There aren't many things in the world that you can still borrow at no charge from non-family members. But you can do that with library books! Sure, they're all previously enjoyed, and some of them have notes in the margins (an act that my sister-in-law Erin, a librarian, thinks is a crime punishable by public flogging), but that's okay. If you go to the library regularly, your child also learns valuable lessons about borrowing and sharing. And you'll save money and storage space. I used to be one of those parents who was too proud to go to a library and liked to buy new books all the time. But I soon changed my tune. All those new books take up about two-thirds of Scarlett's room, while the other third is taken up by stuffed animals. Which brings me to my next dad-dea . . .

Don't buy stuffed animals. It's not that kids don't love them—it's just that this is the classic go-to gift for any toddler. Among the individuals who will show up with a stuffed animal—or as we call it, a stuffie—for your child are the following:

- friends with children
- friends with no children
- thoughtful aunts
- clueless uncles
- distant relatives
- complete strangers

Hell, even the hospital staff sent us home with a stuffed teddy bear after Scarlett was born! Take it from me—if, as a parent, you buy your little one a stuffed animal, you will have officially overstuffed your quota and will rightly face the wrath of your significant other. The problem isn't just the amount of space that the stuffed animals take up (though the room many of them inhabit in our house is my short-lived basement man cave—God rest its soul). What's worse is that some of these stuffies are bigger than the child they were bought for, and very quickly, most of them will have seen better days. I will say that Scarlett has a knack for naming her stuffed toys, though, and it still brings a smile whenever I see them. She has a baby named Grapes, a large dog named Ikea (not purchased at an Ikea store, BTW), bunnies named Danger and Disaster, and a beaver named Static. You would think that given the number of stuffies she has, she wouldn't notice if one or two went missing. But she absolutely would. That's why she's given them names. The most irritating one is a talking penguin whose on/off switch no longer works and whose batteries have run down, so whenever it tries to speak, it basically sounds like a penguin that has had a stroke. Often in the middle of the night, this post-stroke penguin will call out from the bottom of a pile of stuffed toys. And every time, it terrifies me when I hear it. Which leads to my last dad-dea . . .

Don't buy battery-operated toys. I know this advice won't be popular among battery manufacturers, but I'm willing to take my chances. There are a lot of kids' toys out there that are battery-operated—remote-controlled cars, bubble machines, and yes, stuffed animals, to name just a few. I know this because we have a lot of them in our house. But I wish we didn't. Not because they're not fun, or even because they aren't very good for the environment in general (though that's also a good reason, now that I come to think of it), but because there comes a time when they simply don't work anymore. Sometimes a new battery will help, but as time marches on, said toy will eventually give up the ghost. This is especially true for those that contain batteries with a voltage known only to that specific toy manufacturer. (What the hell is an AAAAA 8.5 volt?)

Case in point, Scarlett received from her uncle Phil (the COOL uncle) a toy that was essentially a karaoke kit from the movie *Trolls*. She of course loved it because she's an entertainer's daughter. So what better gift than proper amplification to get used to proper vocal and microphone technique? The twist with this particular gift—which Phil may or may not have known (I'm guessing he KNEW)—is that it also came with a pre-recorded song for kids to sing along with.

And not just any pre-recorded song but a little ditty called "Get Back Up Again." In the movie, this is a charming song belted out by an animated character named Poppy who will not be deterred from saving her village from the dreaded troll-eating Bergens. Apparently the writers came from a family of cannibals. Anyway, Nancy and I smiled as Scarlett sang along to the song the first few times. The song is well over three minutes long, which feels like three weeks when you're really not in the mood to hear it. The next twenty or so times Scarlett sang it, Daddy poured himself a stiff drink the way you would when watching a comedian you don't particularly want to see perform again (I've seen this technique used by many of my friends over the years). Eventually, things started to go a little wonky. The song took on the audio quality of an old cassette tape that had been played too much, even though, as far as I could tell, there was no cassette player inside the toy. I tried to see if the batteries were dying, but I couldn't find an actual battery compartment. So I did what all "handy" husbands do: I handed it over to my wife to fix. But Nancy couldn't find the battery compartment either. So now we had to make a choice: either surreptitiously sneak this toy out of the house (not really an option, since we knew it was on Scarlett's endangered toys list, which meant that it would be the end of the world if this toy disappeared) or let it keep going until it finally didn't make any more noise.

I can't tell you how many more times we had to hear that song. With apologies to the late, great Prince, it's what I imagine doves sound like when they actually cry. After a while, the machine didn't even wait for anyone to activate the song—it would just start itself up with a harsh "HEY! ARE YOU JUST GOING TO SIT THERE? GET UP AND SING!" And then it would go on to torture us in three-minute spurts. The first time this happened was one day when lunch was being prepared and everyone was busily moving around. It was jarring but funny. We all laughed. The second time, it wasn't so funny. I was alone at night in the family room. I had just turned off the TV and was about to turn in for the night. Nancy and Scarlett had been asleep for hours. Even though they were in a bedroom two floors up from me, I was trying my best to be as quiet as possible. I got off the couch and walked across the living room on my way to the kitchen for a glass of water. When I got to the sink, the toy went off with its accusatory "HEY!" I didn't even make it to the second garbled word of the song before I screamed out as if I had just come face to face with Freddy Krueger from *A Nightmare on Elm Street*. I turned in the general direction of where the sound had come from and kicked out with my foot, coming into contact with the solid wood of the toy chest. Which hurt. A lot. So I screamed again. The song just kept going and going, encouraging whoever was listening to keep doing what they were doing. Poppy was saving her village. I was trying to destroy Poppy. I finally found the damn thing in the chest, picked the toy up over my head and smashed it on the ground, stepping on it for good measure.

I really thought I had done it. I had destroyed one of Scarlett's endangered toys. I was already thinking about where I might be able to get my hands on a replacement before she woke up. I'd have to go on the black market for sure. Maybe surf the dark web. Or at least the neighbourhood Facebook page. And that's when I heard it—faint, but still clear. From the very soul of the toy itself came the voice of little Poppy singing the last line of her song: "I . . . will . . . get back up . . . again."

Thank God! It was alive! Poppy was alive! I hugged the toy to my chest like a child who is reunited with a lost puppy or a grown man who finds his missing TV remote.

We still have that toy. It still sings occasionally, I'm sure, but now it's beneath a pile of other toys in the basement. Nancy and I are waiting for the perfect moment to purge our house of it. Poppy hasn't scared the shit out of me in quite a while now, but there are plenty of other battery-powered toys that have.

So do yourself a favour and don't buy them. And if your relatives buy toys like that for your children, support the local economy by hiring the worst dad band you can find to play a full concert outside those same relatives' window at random times in the middle of the night and over several years. Revenge is a dish best served loud and out of tune.

CHAPTER 27

If You Can Learn to Swim, You Can Learn to Dad

I'm not a very strong swimmer. In fact, technically, I can't really swim at all.

For some reason, I was never enrolled in actual swimming lessons as a young child, so I always had to improvise when I was in the water. Elementary school friends would invite me to backyard pool parties and I would sit happily in the shallow end, politely declining all offers to go a little deeper. On rare occasions, I would cling to the side of the pool in the deep end for a few terrifying minutes, and then I would get out of the water and leave the party entirely. After a while, I just declined all invitations to parties that involved pools. Once I got to high school, a couple of friends who were very strong swimmers decided they would teach me how to swim. The lesson was a disaster. They led me to the deep end of a backyard pool, where I panicked and very nearly drowned all three of us. That was enough swimming for me.

In university, I came pretty close to learning how to swim when my friend Melanie, who had been a lifeguard and an actual swim instructor, offered to teach me in the school pool on a weekly basis. The incentive for going to those lessons was the opportunity to see Melanie in a swimsuit. I actually made some progress, though, using things like flippers and flutter boards. But as soon as those things were taken away from me, my ability to swim went right along with them. Plus, I think in the back of my mind, I felt that if I did end up starting to drown, Melanie would be obliged to perform CPR. That was a nicer visual in my mind than actually learning how to master the water. But after several lessons, not only did I not learn how to swim, I never came close enough to drowning to require CPR from Melanie. Idiot!

Then there was the time I went on a white water–rafting trip with some buddies. We were in our early twenties and many of us were headed off to different cities and different life paths after graduation, so it seemed like a good idea to have one more fun trip together. Everyone, of course, knew that I couldn't swim, so we had to take every precaution to ensure my safety. Someone brought along a pair of children's water wings for me. These handy floatation devices are for toddlers who weigh in at about thirty to forty pounds. They are less effective for a full-grown man weighing in at close to two hundred.

In any case, I donned my water wings, paddled through a bunch of rapids, and at some point, floated down the Ottawa River wearing a life jacket. Somehow I stayed alive. As a bonus, I was also one of the few in our group to bungee jump from about two hundred feet up in the air INTO the water below—which would have been terrifying enough if I knew how to swim, but was even more so because I did *not*. I still remember the young guide securing my harness and saying, "Okay, on the count of three, just jump like you're jumping into a pool." I explained to him, "I've never jumped into a pool." Then he replied, "Uh-oh, you're screwed, then," as he laughed and pushed me off the edge. I assume that kid grew up to become a supervillain somewhere.

Fast-forward to the present day, and I *still* have not learned how to swim. This despite having enrolled myself in several public and even private lessons. It's not that I'm afraid of the water. I will put my face under when I'm in a pool or lake. I'm happy to do a front float (even dead bodies can do a front float, so this isn't really much of a feat) and I can also get kicking my legs for a while to move forward. My big move now is to use that flutter board I was introduced to by Melanie a long time ago to keep the front half of my body afloat while I kick my legs out behind me. But I can only do that until the moment I have to breathe. When I bring my face out of the water and turn my head to take a breath, for some reason all hell breaks loose. My kicks (which often come out of the water—a big part of the problem, I know) go out of rhythm and then I start to panic. My feet reach desperately for the bottom of the pool, my heart races, and I stop my imperfect impression of a swimmer. To the casual onlooker, it's probably funnier than anything I've ever done on stage. But it's not funny to me.

If I weren't a dad, I would have abandoned my efforts to learn to swim a long time ago. I am a dad, though, so I keep trying. I have young lives that depend on me, and if those lives depending on me happen to be in water at the time, I need to be at the very least a reliable floatation device for them to hold on to.

To be honest, I'm also kind of ashamed of the fact that I can't swim. All the friends I grew up with know how to do it, and certainly every parent on our block knows. So how the hell is it that I don't?

As much as I would like to blame it on genetics or some sort of physical challenge, it really just comes down to the fact that I was never taught how to swim before I reached an age in which you realize the consequences. Most toddlers and young children think jumping into water is just a fun thing people do. They don't really understand the difference in depth between their home bathtub and an ocean. But once you do know the difference and you don't know how to swim, your mind is drowning in thoughts of . . . well, drowning.

In direct contrast, Nancy, who is a very strong swimmer and even played water polo (a sport that combines treading water while eluding your opponents' attempts to intentionally drown you), got Scarlett into the water as soon as we were able. They enrolled in a tots-and-parents class when Scarlett was a little less than two years of age. Every week, they would go to the pool at the nearby community centre and Scarlett learned to swim by starting with the basics—from blowing bubbles to completely immersing her head in water to the inevitable game of Marco Polo, where one swimmer closes her eyes and yells "Marco" while the others have to say "Polo" while evading her touch. (Note: I have no idea how this activity relates to the thirteenth-century Italian explorer. Maybe the Silk Road region of Asia was prone to flooding? The game should really just be called water tag.)

Could Nancy have taught Scarlett to swim? Yes. But we figured that Scarlett had Nancy's voice in her head for everything else in life, so we might as well bring in an outside voice in this case. (This is the same reason most parents have schoolteachers teach their kids math. Well, that and the fact that a lot of parents are as bad at math as I am at swimming.) Plus, parents of infants and toddlers are always looking to meet other parents of other infants and toddlers, even if it's only during a half-hour swimming lesson. It's just nice to know that there are other people in the world experiencing the same things you are, such as sleep deprivation and anxiety about keeping your baby safe every day.

During Scarlett's lessons, I would go and sit by the side of the pool and wonder to myself, again, "How the hell do I not know how to swim? Little kids are doing it! I'm an adult human of reasonable intelligence. What the hell is wrong with me?" Aren't we *born* surrounded by water in the womb? We live and somehow *breathe* in the water for nine months. How is it that I can't figure out the breathing part of swimming? How did I unlearn that ability along the way? Isn't that technically just forgetting? Why wasn't I taught to swim before I forgot how?

When Nancy enrolled Scarlett in her first tots-only swim lesson, she didn't check with our daughter to see if it was okay—she just did it. And as much as Scarlett hated the first lesson because Nancy wasn't in the water with her, she quickly adapted and learned. (It was a difficult first lesson for Nancy too. Scarlett jumped off the edge of the pool when the instructor's back was turned. We were watching from behind a glass barrier and Nancy very nearly smashed through it to get to her.) Scarlett is now in level 5 of her program and happily jumps in the deep end of any pool, or indeed into any body of water we allow her into. Her proficiency in the water is something for which I'm grateful. But still, it is embarrassing that my five-year-old is a better swimmer than I am. I'm happy that my aqua-incompetence hasn't been passed on. Thank aqua-God (I believe that's King Triton from *The Little Mermaid*).

Meanwhile, at the age of forty-eight, I completed my most recent round of swimming lessons. I was grouped with a small contingent of adults of varying degrees of ability and taught by a teenage instructor (of course) who had a lot of patience but still must have been wondering, "How have these people never learned to swim?" I was actually the only male in the class; the other three students were women in their forties and fifties, who, after raising families, finally had the time to take swimming lessons. One of the women, Naiya, explained that she was taking lessons because she came from a country where "there wasn't much water to drink, let alone swim in." (Well, you win this round of good reasons not to know how to swim, Naiya.)

The program lasted for nine weeks, and although I missed a few classes due to my travel and performance schedule, I definitely improved. I went from avoiding the deep end of the pool to jumping into it (with a floatation belt). I even managed to swim about ten metres to the shallow end. It felt exhilarating. Sure, the thought of jumping into the deep end without that somewhat unfashionable belt still seems as foolhardy to me as running across a rifle range in America dressed as a progressive Democrat, but hey, baby steps.

The thing about swimming, like parenting, is that it's a learned activity. Some people are naturals; others have to work at it. But the only way to get better is to just keep trying. In swimming, they call it stroke improvement as you master your technique and build up your strength. Some people pick up strokes easily, while others struggle with them (hence the expression "Different strokes for different folks," I guess). Some people can tread water for hours, while others can't do it to save their lives. Literally. When I'm treading water (which I'm usually NOT doing), I have to think constantly about the rotation of my legs to make sure they go in the opposite direction. At that point, I usually forget to move my hands as well and start to sink (this is why I have a pool noodle nearby whenever I'm in the water). Some can do front crawl effortlessly, while others (let's call them . . . me) can get out to a good start pushing off the pool wall, but then, once those pesky breathing techniques come into play, will forget everything else and just stop moving. Then there are those who can do all strokes equally well: front crawl, backstroke, breaststroke, sidestroke, diagonal stroke (I think I made that last one up). These people can tread water forever. They are ready for any situation that may arise (except, I suppose, hypothermia: the great equalizer of swimmers and non-swimmers). I admire people like that. I strive to be one of them one day.

For some people, parenting is as natural as breathing (I believe Nancy is one of these people). They instinctively know what to do in every situation. They don't panic because they were taught certain skills early on, and they can call on those skills when they need them. For instance, when Scarlett gets water in her ear after swimming, Nancy knows various techniques for getting it out, while I would just assume you have to live with water in your head for the rest of your life.

Being a dad means the more skills you have, the more you can pass on to your children. And the more important the skill, the more important it is to learn it. I think swimming is an important skill to have, so I *will* learn how to do it, just as I continue to learn how to be a better dad every day. The trick is to improve the parts of parenting that don't come naturally to you until, eventually, they do. Oh, and remember to breathe properly. That's just good life advice in general.

CHAPTER 28

What My Girls Have Taught Me So Far

As a parent, you try to teach your children what to do and, more frequently, what *not* to do. So it's easy to forget that most of the time, your kids are the ones teaching you things. As a dad, it's important to remember this fact so that you can learn some lessons along the way, instead of just doling them out. Here are some of the lessons I've learned from Scarlett, and yes, even baby Norah, so far.

1. Kids Are Essentially Parrots, So Don't Be a Foul-Mouthed Pirate

You may have heard that young kids repeat EVERYTHING their parents say. Before I became a parent, I thought that was an exaggeration, but it's not. It's true. They really do. You are going to have to watch every word you say in front of them. This is particularly challenging in traffic when you are cut off by another (obviously inferior) driver and have to decide how to react. Pre-kids Steve would have said something that sounded a lot like "Duck fou" and then added a gesture that, though made with just one finger, is decidedly different than saying the offending driver is number one. Now, when the kids are in the car, I have to catch myself and turn a harsh swear word into something less harsh. For example, when an inferior driver cut me off in traffic not long ago, I turned my frustration into a cheery song while staring angrily at him: "Fu . . . oooor he's a jolly good felloooooooooow!/Who never learned how to drive!" Scarlett and Norah even sang along.

2. Don't Tell Your Five-Year-Old to Keep Something from Mommy

Maybe it's just because Scarlett is one of the most honest human beings I've ever met (next to her mommy), but whenever I've tried to do something sneaky, like buy her a treat before dinnertime, and have said, "Don't tell your mommy," she has run into the house screaming, "MOMMY! DADDY BOUGHT ME A TREAT!" This is important intel to share with other dads, as you really don't want your kids holding on to classified information for you down the road. Plus, as Nancy has so eloquently pointed out, "There shouldn't be anything that my husband can't tell me!" Fair enough. I guess I have to respect the honesty. Next time, I'll just get a pre-dinner treat for myself and make Scarlett watch me eat it.

3. Little Boys Are Tiny Demolition Machines

I thought it was just me and my brothers who destroyed everything in sight when we were growing up. But Scarlett's little boy friends who have come for play dates have revealed the universal truth: boys love breaking stuff. Just like Bamm-Bamm on the old Flintstone cartoons (if you're a young dad, google it). Each little boy who has visited our home has tried to pull the door of Scarlett's play kitchen off its hinges, has succeeded in removing the legs from her toy barbecue in the backyard and used them as swords, and has inflicted amputations and decapitations on many a stuffed animal. (As you know, I'm not so upset about that.) Fortunately, Scarlett, who is developing fully into a miniature version of Nancy in front of my eyes, usually explains calmly to the boys why their behaviour is wrong while giving a very familiar eye-roll and headshake. I know that look well because it's the same one Nancy gives me whenever I break something in the house.

4. Little Kids Are a Built-in Security System for Your Home

Many parents use the occasion of having children to bump up their home security system, installing sophisticated alarms, bank-vault-calibre locks and motion-sensor lights and cameras. What they don't seem to realize is that they could repel would-be robbers more efficiently and certainly more cost-effectively by simply leaving the front door of the house open with a clear view to what is inside: scattered booby traps of toys in various states of disrepair, and most importantly, NOTHING WORTH STEALING. Believe me. We've tried to get rid of stuff (especially stuffed animals) by leaving it in a box on the curb outside of our house with a sign that says "Free! Please take!" There are never any takers. The only things worth stealing in our house are the clothes that Scarlett and now Norah have inherited from their older cousins, and those tend not to be prime targets for a home invasion. Plus, if you think you can get Scarlett's favourite outfits from her, good luck! I don't care how seasoned a thief you are, she will defend her clothes with the strength of a superhero (many of her favourite outfits are in fact superhero uniforms).Also, the first person a burglar would wake up in our home would be Norah. And trust me, a screaming baby is more effective than any household alarm. Hell, the first time I heard that sound, I ran out of my own house.

5. Early Parenting Is the Most Adorable Form of House Arrest

Simply put, once you have made miniature people from your own DNA, those individuals are the people you will spend most of your time with for the foreseeable future. Before children, if you or your spouse wanted to stay in while the other went out to the pub or a yoga class (it's not important which of these activities is preferred by which spouse), you were free to do so. There was even an option— and this sounds crazy as I'm writing it now—for the two of you to go out . . . TOGETHER! But in the early parenting years, the process of going out is very much like organizing a prison break. You need to map out the escape route, plan for months or years in advance and tunnel out behind the poster of Rita Hayworth that the warden allowed you to have in your cell for doing his taxes. Actually, that's the plot of *Shawshank Redemption*. But it's really not all that different from me trying to get out of the house at night now that I have two young daughters. The only difference is that my struggles aren't narrated by Morgan Freeman.

6. Learning Other Languages Makes You Smarter

Scarlett, who is now a proud graduate of senior kindergarten (or *maternelle*, as it is called by the French School Board of Ontario), is getting very good at understanding and speaking French. I think it's a great skill for a child to learn another language at a young age because it can lead to great life opportunities as she gets older. I have a friend named Juan-Carlos (a good Irish name) who, together with his wife, Jocelyne (Scottish), has two very bright and kind young daughters. Amelie and Eva are perfectly trilingual—they switch effortlessly between English, Spanish and French. Being multilingual is an admirable skill, and it's one that I would love for Scarlett and Norah to have. So while I'm very happy that Scarlett is well on her way to being fluent in French, I just wish she wouldn't correct me every time I try to speak it.

7. It's Okay to Be an Old Dad!

I understand that having children in your middle or late forties isn't ideal. I can see the advantages of becoming a dad in your twenties or thirties. You have more energy, more hair and more years left to make more money that your children will spend more of. But for me, coming to fatherhood later in life has made me appreciate the process much more. While I still have to travel for work, I don't have to travel nearly as much as I used to. And frankly, I couldn't have supported a family in my thirties. (The jury is still out on whether I can do it even now. It depends how well this book sells, I guess.) But I can't imagine not having my girls in my life because they bring me so much joy. They make me work harder now so that I will have more time to spend with them later. (Most likely at the exact time they are ready to spend much less time with me, but still.) Every time they smile or laugh, it makes me happy, no matter how I was feeling immediately before that moment. I'm more proud of every one of my daughters' achievements than I've ever been of any of my own. They make me want to be better every day: a better father, a better husband and a better person. Basically, being an old dad means you might have to try harder than a young dad. But you know what? That's not a bad thing.

CHAPTER 29

Dad Up!

As I woke up this morning for my forty-ninth birthday, I didn't reflect on the fact that I was almost fifty or take stock of what I have achieved or not achieved so far in my life. (One side of that list is a lot longer. It's not important which one.) Instead, I woke up to Scarlett quietly coming into her own room, where I had been sleeping so that she and Norah could enjoy our nice new big bed with Nancy. I was facing away from the door. Scarlett entered the room stealthily, then gently tickled my back to wake me up. This was a sharp contrast from the way she often wakes me up, which is to turn on the overhead light and then dive-bomb onto me. It was a refreshing change, but I know she was holding back only because it was my birthday. A few moments later, Nancy came in holding Norah in one hand and a coffee topped with Baileys Irish Cream in the other. Then all my girls snuggled up to me. A perfect birthday morning.

Eventually, we got out of bed and sat on the floor so I could open my birthday card—homemade, of course, with a very high glitter count. It read, simply, "Happy 49, Love Scarlett." It was worth more to me than any store-bought card (and not just because it used about nine bucks of glitter). Then Norah started to crawl around on the floor, grabbing anything she could get her hands on, so I put her in a laundry basket and started pulling her around the room. This is something that the parenting manuals would probably recommend against for safety reasons, but every dad I know (or at least those who haven't lost touch with their inner child) does this with his baby or toddler (or any age of child that can still fit in a laundry basket) at every opportunity. Norah squealed with delight, Scarlett smiled when I told her how much she used to love doing that exact same thing when she was a baby, and Nancy went down to the kitchen to make my requested birthday breakfast: bacon and cheesy eggs (this dad bod isn't going to maintain itself!).

As I carried Norah down the stairs, yelling after Scarlett with a futile reminder not to run (she didn't hear me because she had already run down the stairs), I looked into my baby's smiling face and made a mental note to remember this moment: my little girls were happy and safe at home with their parents. Then I caught a glimpse of my reflection in the mirror. With my last year in my forties staring back at me, I noticed that my hairline seemed to be receding WHILE I watched.

I'm not sure if all dads have moments of reflection like this.

Are there moments when Slim, now in his late eighties, thinks back to how he once carried his sons down the stairs? Does he still see his little boys when he looks at us as men? Has he ever forgiven nine-year-old me for telling him that I hated him when he pulled me out of a baseball game that he was coaching in order to put in a pinch hitter? (I still think I could have gotten that hit to win the game, by the way.)

Norah won't remember any of this. To her, I am currently a mode of transportation and, on occasion, a warm mattress. I truly believe the first year of being a parent is ALL for you, not for the baby. Sure, you're giving the baby all your love, almost all your attention, and in the case of mothers, life-sustaining nutrition. But really the baby is teaching you. She's teaching you how to be patient, how to find joy at home (because you're not going anywhere for a while) and how to care about another human being more than you do yourself.

Now once your child hits five, she's not a baby anymore. Especially if she has a baby sister in the house. She has to experience the inevitable demotion that comes when her parents' undivided attention now has to be shared. She has to learn to be an older sister, which, from what I've seen so far, is sort of like becoming a second mother. Scarlett is coming into her own, fast. Too fast. All that "it goes by so fast" stuff I talked about before? Damn if it doesn't actually start to make sense! Scarlett is now saying things that are so much wiser than most adults. It makes me wonder, "How is she so smart?" and "How am I so stupid?" Things like, "Daddy, if the gate crew KNEW we were arriving on this plane, why weren't they ready for us when we got here?" When I say it, I'm a sarcastic, impatient arsehole. When she says it, out loud on a crowded plane, it's a very perceptive question.

When I watch my two girls sleeping side by side, reaching for each other in the night, I realize they will always have each other's backs. And that realization makes me very, very happy.

Scarlett knows that with a kiss on Daddy's cheek she gets pretty much whatever she wants.
With Nancy, the proudest mom in the world and a sleeping Norah—a rare photo-op, indeed.
(Photo credit: John Hryniuk.)

Being a dad to my two little girls is my biggest responsibility. Teaching them everything I possibly can is my most important job (and I fully admit, I may have already peaked). And while at times I feel overwhelmed by the responsibility of parenthood and the amount of estrogen in my household, I also feel a sense of exhilaration about what's ahead.

I have so much to look forward to with Scarlett and Norah: coaching them in sports the way my dad coached me (even though I didn't turn out to be a very good athlete), helping them with homework the way my dad helped me (which, to be honest, wasn't that much, but when he did, I liked it) and teaching them the life lessons that he taught me, beginning with "Don't be an arsehole."

Most importantly, I need to remind my girls that they have the most loving mom that they could ever possibly have. Whatever efforts I put into parenting—whatever "sacrifices" I have made to the life I had before I became a dad—they are microscopic compared to what Nancy does every day. When I travel to entertain people, she's home with the girls. When I'm home, it's still Nancy who does the majority of the work. (I am working to be better at that. But hey, this book didn't write itself!) Whatever inner voice told me, "I want that woman to be the mother of my children" was bang on (it sounded like Sir Patrick Stewart, if you're wondering). I've said it before and I'll say it every time I'm asked: the easiest way to be a good dad is to have an amazing spouse beside you—or in my case, waaaaaaay out front, leading the way.

Ultimately, the greatest parents out there don't have time to tell you how to do it. That's because they're too busy (and too exhausted) being attentive parents. So the fact that I have had time to write a whole book about being a dad is a pretty good indication that I have a long ways to go towards being a truly great dad. But I'm trying. Every day, no matter what else is going on in my life—no matter how nervous, anxious, or frankly, frightened I feel for the future—I try to learn a little more. The most important time for me is time spent with my girls, and I will spend every minute that I can with them. It's something I hope to continue doing for many, many years to come. Of course, there will come a day when Scarlett and Norah won't want or need me around. But that day is not today. Today they're here with me, smiling and laughing. Hopefully we're quite a few years off from me getting a mass-produced coffee cup for Father's Day that tells me how special a dad I am. I'd much rather receive a heartfelt note. Or at least a heartfelt book written by a dad who knows that no matter how good a father you are, you can always do better. If you just remember to DAD UP!

Acknowledgements

This book would not have come to be without the editing prowess and patience of Scott "Post-It Notes" Sellers who seemed genuinely surprised to be able to exclaim "We've got a book!" when we finally felt we had one. Or the foresight of my literary agent, Curtis Russell, who had the bold idea that if I could say funny things on stage, perhaps I should write them down and turn them into books.

I also thank my older brothers, John, Larry, Mark and Ross, for always having my back. Except for the one time that I kicked Ross in the front.

It's not lost on me that there is irony inherent in writing a book about parenting, since every moment you are writing is time you are ignoring the children you are supposed to be parenting. Therefore I want to thank my wife, Nancy. Yes it's odd to mention the same person in both the dedication and the acknowledgements, but without Nancy this book wouldn't have been possible. She's been at the centre of all the good things I've enjoyed in my life over the past ten years.

I hope that Nancy enjoys reading this, once she has time to read again, perhaps when Scarlett and Norah have grown up.